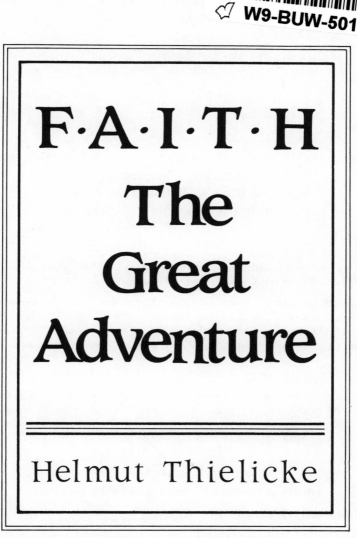

F·A·I·T·H
The
Great
Adventure

Helmut Thielicke

Translated by David L. Scheidt

Fortress Press   Philadelphia

To my colleagues
of the *GLAUBENSINFORMATION* project
in recognition of our ten years
of common labor

This book is a translation from the German *GLAUBEN ALS ABEN-TEUER* (Stuttgart: Quell Verlag, 1980).

Biblical quotations, unless otherwise noted, are from the Revised Standard Version of the Bible, copyright 1946, 1952, ©1971, 1973 by the Division of Christian Education of the National Council of the Churches of Christ in the U.S.A. and are used by permission.

Library of Congress Cataloging in Publication Data

Thielicke, Helmut, 1908–
    Faith—the great adventure.

    Translation of: Glauben als Abenteuer.
    1. Lutheran Church—Sermons. 2. Sermons, German.
I. Title.
BX8066.T46G5713 1985   252'.041   84–48716
ISBN 0–8006–1833–5

1259I84   Printed in the United States of America   1–1833

Contents

iii

Foreword

Life has strange ways of taking us down roads which abound in surprises at every turn and corner. Every day brings something new and different, and we have no way of knowing what it is that will encounter us and cross our path.

At the same time we have a sense of being guided and led through the unknown not by something but by someone who permits that which lies ahead to happen to us. To be sure, this sense of being guided and led through the unknown fills us with suspense and uncertainty. We ask ourselves how the one who leads and guides us can preserve and protect us. We wonder what goal it is toward which he—God—is leading us. So it is that we can speak of being a Christian—of setting out into the unknown under this leading and guidance—as an adventure.

It is about this adventure that I want to meditate with my readers in the pages that follow. By meditation I mean a deeply penetrating reflection which aims at far more than analyzing and understanding something. I mean the kind of reflection by which one opens oneself to the subject at hand and allows oneself to be changed. For this reason I have chosen to meditate here upon a number of biblical texts into which we can grow and which we can leave differently (i.e., changed) than when we came to them.

To this end I have chosen only the kind of texts which (at first glance) appear to have nothing to say to us. Indeed, it would seem that these texts are totally alien and foreign to us. That is precisely why I have chosen them. I intentionally wanted to avoid the usual kind of themes such as faith, hope, and love with which we are all too familiar. Such themes have something of the cliché about them and our very familiarity with them suggests that they hold no adventure in store for us.

As a preacher I realize that often I have hesitated to deal with the kind of texts I have chosen here. I used to say to myself, "If this text says nothing to me, how can I persuade my congregation that it has something to say to them?" Long experience has taught me that if I just keep on trying and do not give up, it is precisely just such difficult texts that yield undreamed-of treasures. I hope that the reader will have the same experience that I have had.

By meditating on a text I mean that we should open ourselves to it in such a way that it permeates our whole being. This is possible only when a text not only touches our person and heart but strikes home at our situation. In other words, the text has to have something to do with our hopes and fears, our emotional heights and depths, our friendships and enmities, our loves and our hates. In other words, a text can become ours when it can be identified with our lives. That does not mean that we are free to contemporize and alter the text as we will. Such alteration would be patently transparent and have a contrary effect. The preacher who would so alter a text would be guilty of substituting his own spirit for that of the Lord. I sincerely hope that I have not been guilty of this; I sincerely hope that these texts speak to us and find their dwelling place in our thought.

The meditations which follow have grown out of my work with the German Christian publication *Glaubensinformation*. To the colleagues who share in that project I dedicate this volume and thank them for all they have given and mean to me.

HELMUT THIELICKE

PART ONE

GOD AS THE LORD
OF OUR LIFE

CHAPTER 1

The Business of Spiritual Training

Look carefully then how you walk, not as unwise men but as wise, making the most of the time, because the days are evil. Therefore do not be foolish, but understand what the will of the Lord is. And do not get drunk with wine, for that is debauchery; but be filled with the Spirit, addressing one another in psalms and hymns and spiritual songs, singing and making melody to the Lord with all your heart, always and for everything giving thanks in the name of our Lord Jesus Christ to God the Father. Be subject to one another out of reverence for Christ.

Eph. 5:15–21

A few years ago I had the great privilege of visiting a renowned master of Zen Buddhism in his temple in Japan and of engaging him in lengthy theological discussion. That was by no means an easy matter, for somehow we had to find a common ground on which to meet and engage in dialogue. As a Christian theologian I was conditioned by certain theological ideas and concepts which have come to us in varied traditions down through the centuries. I should have discussed some of these ideas with the master of Zen: his concept of man, evil, grace, justification, etc. But my Buddhist colleague knew nothing of such matters. He was so immersed in contemplation and meditation that he was beyond all such concepts. Indeed, my Japanese counterpart was even beyond language itself. Of course, he was too much of a gentleman to tell me that my concepts and ideas were utterly superfluous, whereas Zen exercises and meditation penetrate into man's total being and that of the cosmos. That kind of immersion released powers and abilities far superior to those which can be developed and unleashed by an athlete's rigid training. He and I, however, did find a common ground on which to confront each other, namely in our understanding of man. Over against the Zen Buddhist position that man is ultimately absorbed into the great All (just as all streams and rivers and oceans merge into one), I had to argue that man is redeemed at a price. I had to uphold the idea that by being so redeemed man is called by his name.

Quite honestly I must say that I was impressed by my Zen colleague, but I was not won over to his point of view. I did, however, come to the conclusion that this man had something at his disposal which Christians, alas, largely lack—that silent immersion into oneself which we call meditation. He lived and breathed what he understood to be an authentic reality. Do we who call ourselves Christians and say that we are "in Christ" do the same? Or do we not rather concern ourselves (especially we theologians) with intellectual mastery or sentimental relationship to the Lord? Do we know anything of what could be called a spiritual exertion to live and breathe "in Christ" such as this Zen Buddhist devotes to his All-One?

Could it be—and it is with this thought in mind that I took leave of that Japanese sage—that our Christian faith has room for immersion in meditation such as that to which the wise old master of Zen had devoted himself? Our text gives us important hints toward answering this question.

The pietists of another day and age had an expression that sums up what I have been trying to say. That expression is *cultura animi*, the training of the soul.

To be sure, such an expression can suggest a kind of spiritual arrogance. But does it also point to something, the lack of which I became so painfully aware of after my conversation with the old Zen master? The question put to us here is this: must we not protect our Christianity, our spiritual man from inner bankruptcy? That is to say, must we not lead the spiritual man beside still waters and to green pastures instead of letting him starve and wither? Is not our faith a possession once won for us, something we must not lose through our carelessness? I am certain we all know examples of just such carelessness and neglect. We all know of examples of how the inner life dries up and withers, of how prayer dies out and our hearts know no thankfulness and a spiritual bankruptcy sets in.

This bankruptcy is not something that happens in some obvious way. We do not shout for all to hear that God and Christ are just stories from antiquity which have no meaning for our life which we renounce once and for all. Rather, our bankruptcy takes place as George Bernanos describes it in his novel, *The Diary of a Country Parson*. There he writes: "One does not lose faith; one just stops giving any shape or form to life." Faith is in no way consciously abolished from our lives; faith is just relegated to an obscure cranny of our minds. There is danger of such bankruptcy in every life. That is why our inner life has to be cultivated.

It is precisely to this theme that the author of the Epistle to the Ephesians (either Paul himself or, more likely, one of his disciples) turns our attention. The author starts from the point of view that faith is in very great danger and that it is very doubtful that we will endure "to the end" (Matt. 10:22). It is not Christ who is in doubt but our faith. So it is that Luther could say: "It is most certain that Christ has redeemed us by his blood. But for your sake it is not certain." Our faith can fall apart because of the same daily routine.

This is what the author of Ephesians means when he speaks of evil days. Repeatedly we hear in our day the demand that the church must be relevant and preach relevantly. Obviously there is legitimacy to this demand. After all, if the gospel did not speak the language of our day and to its needs, if the gospel had no meaning for our marriage and the education of our children, and did not confront us in the news we read in the daily paper, and did not give us ground under our feet and direction to what we see and experience, then the gospel would be powerless. Indeed, that gospel would have become a food that does not feed or strengthen the soul. To be sure, such a gospel may give us a moment of uplift, but it does not make Christ the Lord of our life. On the contrary, such a gospel shuts Christ out of our life and makes him an outsider. No, dear reader, there is a tremendous and fundamental difference between being contemporary and being relevant. Indeed, what does it mean to be relevant? Why are the times for which we pre-scribe evil times?

The gospel speaks about the "ruler of this world." In speaking further of this ruler Scripture (Eph. 2:2; 6:12; Peter 5:8; cf. also John 14:30) also says that the devil goes about like a roaring lion. To be sure, certain "progressive" theologians are doing their best to empty hell and to send the devil into retirement as a mythical fright figure. It is rather shameful that it took a Marxist philosopher, Leszek Kolakowski, to point out to Christians that they are seriously mistaken and fall prey to illusions when they try to do away with such figures as the devil. Even in horror movies and films about exorcism and demons and the like we sense that when all is said and done there is something to this business about the powers of darkness.

What does our text have in mind when it alludes to the power of darkness which makes ours an evil time? Does not this expression mean that the spirit of our times produces temptations which seek to inject our faith life with deadly germs?

And to what does "being drunk with wine" refer? Does it not remind us that we can fill our souls with things that leave no room for serious thoughts or faith? It is a demanding and exhausting business to concentrate on the "one thing . . . needful" (Luke 10:42); it requires a tremendous amount of self-discipline. On the contrary, however, it is an easy thing to let one's thoughts fly off into all kinds of intoxication. One needs only to submit to every professional stress that assails us, to put on a rock record in every free moment, or to stare endlessly into the "boob tube." Indeed the excessive use of alcohol does not play an insignificant role. Drinking offers us forgetfulness but does nothing to help overcome our pressures and conflicts. Drinking is like taking the wrong medicine at the wrong time. At first alcohol gives emotional satisfaction and fulfillment; but then comes the hangover!

That is why we should pay attention to how we live and to what we do for recreation. We need to ask ourselves, Does our recreation really help us to refresh ourselves without having a hangover or rude awakening to follow? The answer is no if all we are concerned about is just a momentary thing that becomes a lasting condition. Even good and godly things can separate us from God and destroy our inner life so that we become so dependent upon them that we make them into gods and confer upon them the ultimate value of deity. The question that confronts us is this: Do we want to cover up the emptiness of our lives with meaningless and fraudulent fillers or do we want that peace bestowed upon us which is a reserve of strength for the daily conflicts and struggles of our life?

Our text says that we should make the most of the time. In Galatians (3:13; 4:5) Paul uses the term "redeem" in the sense that Christ ransoms us and makes us free. But we can redeem or free ourselves from the times only when we pay the necessary price. But we have no control over that price. We cannot simply decide to be free of this or that, as any drug addict or alcoholic can readily attest. If we are a vacuum it is because the spirit of the times has entered into us and met with no resistance. It is only when we receive Christ and have the good fortune to know his presence, companionship, and guidance that we can resist the things that masquerade as happiness and all we need. We are always filled with something—either the substance of eternity or of the present. And one excludes the other!

If we see things this way, then it is clear to us that when our text says "look carefully" and "understand" it does not mean that we already understand what is involved on the basis of our Christian education or having listened to sermons. Our text means rather that from henceforth we must take heed of ourselves and persevere. It is as though the text were asking if we were ready to confront new miracles and trials every day. To be a Christian is an adventure, and Christians must be resigned to a life of surprises.

Furthermore, we should be greatly mistaken if we understood our text in so rigid and moralistic a sense that we could never forgive ourselves anything. And it is precisely that forgiving against which one would have to be scrupulously on guard. That would be a downright perversion of the training of the soul and lead to pointless legalistic dilemmas and senseless contemplation. This business of looking carefully—of paying heed—means not so much to be concerned about what we do as with why we do it: if we go along with what the Lord wants or instead go on strike and stand on the sidelines. "Set your minds on things that are above . . ." (Col. 3:2). There is a tremendous freedom in what we do. Everything is ours, but we are Christ's (cf. 1 Cor. 3:23). Our freedom is exercised in this tie to the Lord.

In other words, we are called upon to keep this motive in mind: we belong to the Lord. Whoever stands firmly on this ground will not stumble and fall. It is for this that our souls should be trained, and such training does not require all manner of ascetic undertakings.

Giving thanks is an example of that training of the soul to which we are exhorted, for giving thanks is not something we can do once and for all; it is a daily matter. To give thanks is good for us because whoever does so is not forever bogged down in the temporal and everyday but rises above today. Such a person fixes his or her mind on all that is lovely as well as what is harsh and difficult. At the same time such a one fixes his or her mind on life's goal and what it is the Lord wants with us. That alone is what confers peace.

It may strike us as peculiar that our text confronts us with challenges and demands over which we have no power. What then does it mean when our text calls upon us to be filled with the Spirit? Is the Spirit not a gift which is at our disposal—or is it? One never knows from whence the Spirit comes or whither it goes (John 3:8). Must not one wait until the Spirit comes? And if the Spirit does not come? Then we are God's stepchildren; faith is denied us. It just is not in our power to lay hold of the Spirit for ourselves. These are the kinds of questions that encounter us here and they make us shake our heads in wonder.

Obviously one cannot give himself the Spirit of God—the Spirit must be given to us. Yet there is something we can do: we can pay scrupulous heed to what stands in the way of the Spirit's coming to us, to why it is we impede the Spirit's coming to us by our behavior. Whoever prefers newspapers and magazines, with their overabundance of information and pictures that do nothing but help to kill time, to immersing oneself in the Bible, that person has no excuse to say that the Spirit of God could find him if he (the Spirit) wanted. Whoever has not entered the fellowship of Christians or has never heard or sung hymns or Psalms erects a barrier to the Spirit. Whoever exploits his neighbor for his own ends and cares nothing for him, who will not serve his neighbor as Christ serves us (Matt. 20:28; Luke 22:26) has locked himself into an inner taciturnity. Perhaps he has all kinds of doubt which he attributes to an intellect that is too critical to accept dogmas when in fact

these doubts grow out of a wrong attitude toward life. Our conduct
has already built up an antipathy to faith and belief and we employ
our intellect to silence the demanding and insistent voice of conscience. This is what Paul means when he speaks of quenching
(literally "stifling") the Spirit (1 Thess. 5:19).

Everything I have spoken of here as an impediment to receiving
the Spirit is indicated in our text. Our text says what our lives must
be like if we want our hearts prepared to receive the Spirit. By the
same token our text also shows us what life is like when it is her-
metically sealed against the Spirit. Quite rightly the text calls upon
us to take heed because we can both make something of our receptivity and miss a great deal. For example, the text advises us to
nurture Christian fellowship, which implies that we should discuss
with each other questions of faith. Even the joy expressed in singing
belongs to this. Christians should include the Lord in everything
that occupies them in all of life. Permit me to cite three examples
of how this including the Lord in everything has made its impression on my life.

1. Julius Schniewind, a renowned New Testament scholar, was
one of my teachers, and we students thought the world of him. He
often took part in our monkeyshines so that we thought of him
more as an older brother or friend than as the foreboding "Herr
Professor" of the lecture platform. But somewhere along the line
there was always a turning point which went something like this:
"Well boys, we have had a lot of fun together. But our time together
is very brief, and we should not lose the opportunity to speak of
Jesus." That great scholar (and fine pianist) was not embarrassed
to come down to our level to talk with us—whether at an open
house at his home or in private conversation—to lead us to him
who is the source of life.

2. I had been on a lecture series, which had lasted for several
weeks, for students near Los Angeles. At the end of these edifying
and (humanly speaking) invigorating and pleasant sessions there
was a masquerade party. Each of us was supposed to wear some
kind of comical headgear at dinner that evening. You never saw
such a display in your life! As we took our places at table—still
wearing out hilarious headgear—a table prayer was spoken. As we
bowed our heads our headgear produced an odd collection of

sounds—chiming, ringing, clacking, clinking, etc. It was so comical that I found it difficult to be serious enough to speak the table blessing. My dinner companions looked at me with amazement and as nicely as I could I said: "Sometimes you Americans are really strange people. First you have a masquerade party and then you pray. We Europeans are no longer naive enough for that. But I admit that it is a question of style which is highly debatable." The people at my table were flabbergasted at my astonishment. "Why," they asked, "should we not ask the Lord to be present when we are having fun? Do we let him in only at official services of worship? Should we celebrate as heathen?" I confess that I was ashamed of myself for feeling so superior. Ever since then I have made a point—no matter how much I may joke with my students—of reading or leading them in the singing of a hymn as a reminder that there is nothing in life in which we cannot involve the Lord.

3. There are always among us those stiff-backed, straightlaced folks who crave fixed, unchanging form and style. They are the kind of people who become very upset with younger members of the congregation who are not content with organ music and the traditional hymns but want to have jazz and rock and dance music (indeed, dancing!) in the services. Should we not be happy when young people introduce the musical styles they prefer and rejoice that they identify God with things that are a part of them? Everyone must have the right to praise God with his own voice. We can sing only that song that is a part of us, and only when we sing that song do we include the Lord in our lives.

Our text does not tell us to immerse ourselves in the secrets of faith, of heaven, hell, and the afterlife. Nor does our text say: Do what is right; fear no man; be content with Christian deeds. Rather, what our text wants to say is this: Let your faith and life be one wherever you may be. And by all means be no stranger where one hears the sounds of faith, where Christian believers hear the word of life and wait upon the same spirit. "Jesus is my life and light" sings an old German hymn, and that is true. Jesus Christ is our life and light. The question is, Do we walk in that light? Certainly I can hobble around in life's darkness, torn to shreds by its griefs and muddled thinking until suddenly I discover that I am old and terrified by the emptiness of my life. I must, as Luther put it, break out of my house of darkness. And here is where the imperatives of our text come to bear. The apostle gives us to understand how filled our lives can be. He who opens his life to the spirit of God is most fortunate and happy. He is on his way to becoming what the Lord has in mind for him and his peace is total and complete. Loneliness must leave us because we have brothers and sisters in the Lord. All the challenges, directions, and admonitions of our text have the single point that every day we should return to the spring of life and drink its waters. Here we should be trained as guides who no longer wander about in darkness and confusion, but who keep our eye upon our goal in the certainty that we are on the right path.

Two Kinds of Christianity: Word and Deed

What do you think? A man had two sons; and he went to the first and said, "Son, go and work in the vineyard today." And he answered, "I will not"; but afterward he repented and went. And he went to the second and said the same; and he answered, "I go, sir," but did not go. Which of the two did the will of his father? They said, "The first." Jesus said to them, "Truly, I say to you, the tax collectors and the harlots go into the kingdom of God before you. For John came to you in the way of right-eousness, and you did not believe him, but the tax collec-tors and harlots believed him; and even when you saw it, you did not afterward repent and believe him.

Matt. ~~28:~~21:28–32

It always annoys me when ministers scold and berate their con-gregations on particularly beautiful Sundays when church attend-ance is poor and people are more drawn to the golf courses, moun-tains, and beaches than to God's house. Almost always the preachers are criticizing the wrong people. The ones to whom what they are saying is really addressed are beyond the sound of their voice. But that was not the case with the Bible stories we call parables. In these stories it is the pious pew warmers who come under criticism. So, then, instead of hearing others roundly censured here, it is we ourselves who come under criticism. Or, to employ the allusion of another Gospel story, we are not dealing with the splinter in our neighbor's eye but with the beam in our own.

The Bible has many such stories. For instance, there is the Parable

11

of the Great Banquet (Luke 14:16 ff) in which the Lord speaks about those who have been called—the baptized, the enlightened, those to whom the gospel has been preached and to whom it makes sense—and yet, in the decisive moment it is they who falter and fall. I think of Jesus' accusation of the holy city when he said: "O Jerusalem, Jerusalem, killing the prophets and stoning those who are sent to you! How often would I have gathered your children together as a hen gathers her brood under her wings, and you would not!" (Luke 13:34). Here blessing becomes accusation and judgment.

Finally, there is the example of Jesus' rebuke of those cities in which great and godly acts had been performed and yet those cities did not repent. If those same works had occurred in Sodom and Gomorrah those cities would still be standing. Indeed, Jesus said, it will go better on the day of judgment with those two cities of antiquity than it will with those ten cities upon which God had showered his goodness in such abundance (Matt. 11:20–24).

Certainly there is more than just "moral censure" in Jesus' words. These are words of pain and sorrow in the deepest sense. And what greater pain and sorrow can there be than when one has done so very much for another, at incalculable cost to oneself, only to receive a cold shoulder in return? Johann Walter's great patriotic hymn "Awake, O German Land, Awake" is an example. In this hymn the German nation is called upon to remember and call to mind all the the goodness God had bestowed upon its land and people through the years. And beyond the poet's recital of divine beneficence there hovers the question: What have you done with all you have received?

Perhaps God's pain is due to the numerous defections from the church in our day. Certainly the decline in church membership statistics cannot make him happy. But to my way of thinking, is not God more sorrowful and pained about what his people have missed than he is about membership statistics? Is he not more pained and grieved by the emptiness and shallowness of so much of our church life, that makes being a Christian seem dull and unattractive?

Our text speaks of God's sorrow for his people. Here it is not a case of the Lord giving directions to hired hands. Rather he is speaking as a father to his sons about his—their—vineyard and about the jobs each has to do. The father has reared his sons with love. He has worked his fingers to the bone so that they would take to the soil which he would one day give to them to be their own. This is why he assigned his sons chores as though they were servants. If the sons refused to accept the tasks which he assigns them, then their refusal constitutes not only a dereliction of duty but a contempt for their father's love.

What makes people act like those sons in our text? The second son says "Yes, Father, I'll do as you say." But then he reneges on his promise. His saying yes is just so much hot air. His yes is, at best, halfhearted. But his yes is also a "yes, but," so that in effect he is saying "I'll do what you want, but first I have to go to a funeral"; or "I have to inspect something I just bought"; or "I have some very personal matters to which I must attend. Once I have my personal affairs in order, then I can give myself to the business of discipleship and the inner life [Matt. 8:21; Luke 14:18–20]. I will follow, but only with reservations. There are certain aspects of my life over which I must keep a free hand." Money, career, sex, and much, much else come under this reservation clause of "yes, but."

The young man really wants to go to work in the vineyard, so it is really not a base act of deception when he says yes but does not do what he said he would do. As long as he has things in mind which he considers more important then his yes simply recedes more and more into the background until it is completely stifled and forgotten.

The person who is satisfied to say yes is usually one of those spontaneous people who says yes very quickly, without giving too much thought to the matter. We see this most clearly in people like the Jesus-people who are emotionally aroused and touched by certain kinds of preaching and sermonizing. I was sitting next to Billy Graham at one of his rallies and I was very impressed how, after the sermon, hundreds of worshipers, under the very moving influence of the choir's singing, pressed forward to respond and say yes to the call to discipleship. As I took in the sight of all this I wondered if these people realized what they were doing. Had they really counted the cost of discipleship? Had they really taken into consideration the kind of conflicts into which their yes would bring them? Only gradually does it dawn on them what this yes of their's involves. Jesus has begun something with them and he wants to carry it to completion in every phase of their lives. He compels changes in their lives. Moreover he has great significance for every aspect of their lives: their marriage, their relationship to their children, their professional lives. They may be convinced that they have said their yes to Jesus and have been converted. But their whole being has not yet been stirred and reached by what has touched the heart.

So the second of these two sons thinks to himself that he will go to work in the vineyard. But on the way to the vineyard it dawns on him that there is more to this than just a healthy walk. It dawns on him that it will get very hot around noon (when he said yes the morning was still cool and it was easy to say yes). It becomes clear that the people who work in the vineyard have all kinds of squabbles and gripes. It will not be an easy matter for each to get his own way. Moreover there are transportation problems, quarrels with the neighbors. You see, the one son turns aside from all that "and" that is involved with saying yes, and he heads for a cool and shady spot where he can take his ease in comfort. He is one of those people of whom Jesus says: They say "Lord, Lord" and "yes, yes" to him. But he does not know them. Their deeds have negated their words [Matt. 25:12].

This business of saying yes but then doing the direct opposite is what Jesus calls hypocrisy. The hypocrite does not intentionally pretend to be something other than what he is. Nor does the son in our text. He honestly intended to do what he told his father he would do. Jesus understands hypocrisy to be a conscious and deliberate self-contradiction about which the hypocrite himself—for the most part—is not clear.

The Sermon on the Mount (Matt. 5:23) speaks of just such a person. There Jesus tells us of a man who says yes to God and in token of his yes he wants to lay an offering on the altar. But this man is not in a right relationship with his neighbor. To his neighbor he is saying no. As he makes his way to the temple, there to lay his gift, the thought never once occurs to him that he could become involved in a contradiction. Jesus has to provide clarification. He knows our hearts better than we ourselves. So Jesus tells him: As long as you have not purified your heart and made peace with your neighbor you are contradicting your word to God by what you do. Your word means nothing, so then, yes is not always yes.

That is dissembling. Jesus said the same thing about swearing (Matt. 5:37).

Now we come to the son who at the outset had said no. The other son had said yes and he had emphasized his assent by saying, "I go, sir." The first son spoke his no without saying anything else. In a sense the father no longer exists as far as he is concerned because the father has no place in the son's heart. He is, as it were, an atheist who does not protest against God or try to come to an understanding with him. If one does that one is taking God seriously. The first son ignores his father. Yet he actually does go to the vineyard, thereby refuting what he says by what he does. It is clear that Jesus meant that while the tax collectors, harlots, and heathens may speak no "yes" to God, nonetheless they come closer to his heart than do all the pious "Lord, Lord" babblers.

How do we recognize such people today? Who are they? Are they the ones we call activists, the movers and shakers of our day, the people who change society? Or are they the secular humanists who jettison all the luggage of dogma and who abandon theologians for the practical men of action? I often wonder if these are not the ones of whom it is said that they "are not far from the kingdom of God" (Matt. 12:34). Is it not so like God that at the final judgment we shall have abundant reason to marvel at who will be among the sheep and who among the goats (Matt. 25:32)? Certainly many of these activists and practitioners of practical help—the ones who say no to God—will hear the Lord acknowledge them as having been the ones who visited him when he was in prison, who fed him when he was hungry, and who clothed him when he was naked. How many who said their no will recognize him and fall reverently to their knees before him whom they once had seen only as a neighbor who turned to them for help (Matt. 25:34 ff).

Still, all of this does not capture in full the son who says no.

What does the gospel mean when it speaks of people who keep saying no and yet who do the Father's will? Does it not mean the Good Samaritan, who saw in that beaten and battered fellow lying in the road the one to whom he had to be a neighbor (Luke 10:30)? Certainly the Samaritan knew something of a God of love, but he had not said his yes to this God as had the priest and the Levite, who had taken solemn vows of ordination. Yet these two—priest and Levite—passed the injured man and let him lie there injured and helpless. They were just like the second son in our text. The Samaritan had not given his yes, but nonetheless he did the godly work of compassion. Even that other Samaritan, the only one of those ten lepers whom Jesus had healed who returned to give thanks (Luke 17:16), had not said his yes to Jesus. And yet that Samaritan was deeply grateful to the Lord for his act of kindness to him. Both of these Samaritans had heard the note of the gospel. To be sure, they did not know from whence that note was sounded, but they were certainly close to the heart of God even though they had not confessed their faith in some formal way. God permits himself to be found by whomever this note is heard and followed (Matt. 7:8).

Then there was the Canaanite woman (Matt. 15:22). If someone had shown her a confession of Christ that conformed to the catechism and asked her if this was what she believed and confessed she would have shaken her head in confusion and ignorance. Such a confession would have been all Greek to her. She knew nothing of the Holy Scripture nor the catechism nor any Christian confession based on them. Furthermore, she was not acquainted with the gospel Jesus preached and made known. But this we do know— she had grasped the groundswell of trust which is at the bottom of faith. She did not let what appeared to the contrary discourage her but rather she held fast to her trust and said "but yet."

What is it about such people? They do not say yes, but yet they come close to God's heart, bringing him their love and trust and gratitude. It is not that their good deeds make them saints.

But what is it that moves their heart? How is it that God hears them say yes even when they are saying no and are unable to make a "proper" Christian confession? For the answer to that we must look again to the first son in our text. The fact that he had a change of heart and went off to the vineyard after he had said no has to be because he remembered something. He remembered that it was his father who asked him to do this work. His father's face kept coming into his mind. All his father had done for him! Could he not do at least this little chore for his father? Could he just turn his back on his father's request?

I suspect that it was the memory of his father that led this son to have a change of heart. The decisive word in our text is not that the son went into the vineyard despite having said he would rather not, but rather the remark that he was sorry for what he had said. How could he come to this regret unless he remembered whom he had injured with his no? Did not even the Canaanite woman sense from afar that God's heart is not untouched when a human being turns to him in boundless trust?

I often wonder if those who in our day regard themselves as secular humanists do not act on the basis of just such faint recollections of the Father and for that reason they may well be closer to the hour of repentance than we think. From where else do they get their ethic of the practical love of neighbor, their readiness to help handicapped children, to aid the elderly and the sick? Certainly this ethic can hardly be motivated by the intention of seeing to it that there are only useful members of society. After all, everyone who thinks only in economic terms—what is the value of it—must conclude it has no value. Whence comes this canonization of the "human" which is not concerned about bottom-line results but rather respects the dignity of the individual and cares for life that is unfit to live—for cripples, the old and shaky, the mental cases? Does not such respect come from the remembrance that we have been bought at a price (1 Cor. 6:20) and this price was paid for the poorest and least worthy? Was not the one who told the parable of these two sons the one who brought us the news that this price was paid?

If one were to put these questions to many of these so-called humanists they would be embarrassed. You could ask them, for example, why do you not use the term "unfit for life"? Just because the Nazis used the term? Surely there must be another way of putting these people out of their misery. Who is so concerned about another and his dignity? We would have to say to the humanist that though he does not recognize the Christ, yet he has said his yes to him, and this will be confirmed on judgment day. For that reason it may well be said of him that he is "not far from the kingdom of God." Indeed, he may put to shame many who shout their yes loudly and clearly for all to hear, but they will never go on the road where they are encountered by the hungry and the thirsty, the exploited and the drained, the oppressed and the depressed who cry out for help.

CHAPTER 3

We Are a Letter from God, Not an Advertisement

Paul writes: "Are we beginning to commend ourselves again? Or do we need, as some do, letters of recommendation to you, or from you? You yourselves are our letter of recommendation, written on your hearts, to be known and read by all men; and you show that you are a letter from Christ delivered by us, written not with ink but with the Spirit of the living God, not on tablets of stone but on tablets of human hearts.

"Such is the confidence that we have through Christ toward God. Not that we are competent of ourselves to claim anything as coming from us; our competence is from God, who has made us competent to be ministers of a new covenant, not in a written code but in the Spirit; for the written code kills, but the Spirit gives life."

2 Cor. 3:1–6

I once suggested a title to a publisher which used the word "church." "Forget it," the publisher advised, adding, "Even people who believe in God and are sympathetic to Christianity are not very excited about the church and its personnel. One has too many unhappy experiences with them." If that is true and the church does encounter all kind of antipathy and hostility, one thing is certain: the problem is not caused by the clash with the so-called modern world. Men of God are always controversial people. Take Paul for example. In Corinth there were those who doubted that he was a genuine apostle. They accused him of arrogating undue power to his office. Similarly, people ask our church what gives it the right to speak and act as it does. By what right, many ask, does the church say what it says on matters such as abortion, divorce, equal opportunity, public and private property, to name just a few of the questions dealt with in statements and resolutions issued by the church and its agencies? By what right, people ask, does the church claim to know the sense and meaning of life and seek to impose its viewpoint on others as binding? Those who are critical of the church (are we among them?) are not critical of the church's ability to become involved in worldly matters which have nothing to do with the church. Rather, the objection asks what gives the church the right to say what it says in the name of God. After all, the church is just one of many voices which address themselves to the pluralistic society of our day. But the church speaks with a voice of absolute truth, acting as though what it says came straight from heaven. The church's critics claim that the church clothes its clergy in special garb in order to make its privileges visual. Moreover—at least this is the case in much of Europe—there is the criticism that the church is not just a corporation but a special and favored corporation. What right does the church have to all of this? This is a very ticklish question, and to use the jargon of the day, the church has to ask how it can commend itself best to its contemporaries. Paul faced that question in Corinth. How did he deal with it?

To get at the contrast between ourselves and Paul we have to ask how we permit our contemporaries to identify us. Then we see and hear how affirmations of loyalty abound in our church against everything that is modern and progressive. We use every means— from modern jargon and idioms right down to jazz and rock music— to try to make it clear that the church understands modern man, especially youth. Because sociopolitical programs are so "in and up-to-date" (here I myself use "in" and modern expressions of speech), we speak of the gospel as though it were a revolutionary ideology. Furthermore, we do not fail to recommend the cultural-political significance of Christianity for the Western world as well as the social and political significance of social ministry.

Does Paul speak in such terms? It could be that he comes very close to doing so. He says to his people: You are my letter—my letter of recommendation—indeed, you are even more than that: you are a manuscript by Christ himself.

What does Paul mean by that? Does he want to say people have only to look at Christians to be convinced of Paul's cause? "Like Father, like son," as the old expression puts it. You are the offspring of the heavenly Father, and I, as his earthly representative, am recommended to you.

Are we God's brand? Do we carry his trademark? One has to say this in a rather crude way in order to realize immediately that this is not what Paul means—when the claim is disproved every day by our patent and de facto wretchedness.

Now a letter has two characteristics. First, a letter is addressed to someone. We are like a letter God wants to make known and to send to our contemporaries. Second, a letter contains something the recipient should read and understand.

And now for the real question: Can our fellow men respect us and the one who sent us? Can they read in us the message God wants to send through us? Or are we just so much junk mail that is earmarked for the wastebasket? Nietzsche had something like that in mind when he said that Christians should look more saved than do the rest of us if he was to believe in their savior. Do we not have the feeling that we fail to come up to our own advertising, that we should be returned to the company and the customer's money be refunded?

There are people who will never permit themselves to be bound by anything in writing. But God has done just that. He has committed himself in writing. Now it depends on what he has put into writing. Certainly what he put into writing cannot say "Examine my product . . . My best recommendation . . . commended to your imitation." We have already noted that. But what, then, does this letter that we are have to say? It says two things.

First, God's missive says that the man or woman who is his letter does not want to be his (or her) own master but believes God when he says "I am the Lord your God" and recognizes his (or her) wretched unworthiness. Such a person trusts that God will not abandon him or her, that God is his or her rod and staff in the valleys of the shadow, his or her solid ground in anxiety and the source of joy in life's high hours.

Second, this letter revokes the indebtedness which hangs over our life and declares our debt null and void (Col. 2:14). The Epistle to the Colossians knows full well that we are no great advertisement for God. Nonetheless God accepts us and rejects the application for the refund for which those who are dissatisfied with us have applied. Our note of indebtedness is nullified and cancelled. The new letter which we now are is written across the back of the old money-back guarantee. Our consciences tell us what that means. The people around us have underlined the word "dissatisfied," have seen what we are and our deficiency more clearly than we ourselves. God has written across our note of indebtedness the words "Paid in full. The debt is cancelled."

I am this kind of letter, too. I am not a letter of recommendation for my firm but rather a certificate that I am accepted by my firm, employed by it, and that the firm stands behind me regardless of all my shortcomings, all of which I must admit are true.

Of course, we know that no business firm in the world would write such a letter. The letter which gives this assurance of faithfulness is unique and without parallel; it is the documentation of a miracle that just does not happen in the business world. But it pledges that the God of the godless himself takes over our debt. The gospel—that is what it is all about—does what no human pledge or promise makes.

If we want to be designated as a letter of God we cannot claim that we are letters of recommendation because the letter is not about us. The letter speaks about realities and circumstances that lie beyond us and our ability and that is clear to us from three points of view.

First, if we as the church are to be this letter of Christ, then is it not to be understood as a gathering of religiously and ethically responsible personalities? Rather, is the church of Christ much more a matter of people who have been gathered about a message which they themselves did not create—the message that we are loved and that there is nothing which can so alienate us from the Father that it can prevent him from accepting us as his own?

Second, when an individual is designated as the letter of Christ it is not because the individual is a member or pillar of the church but rather because he or she is the bearer of what Luther called the "strange dignity." By that Luther meant the opposite of everything we call our own, for example, our ability to function in our own profession or in some social endeavor. Our dignity is strange or alien because it is grounded in what God (one who is other, i.e.,

alien) has done for us, what he has applied to us, and that by which
he has bought us with a great price (1 Cor. 6:20; 7:23).

Third, if I as a preacher of the gospel were supposed to be such
a letter, it would not be because I am learned in scripture or because
I have special insights and am a professor of faith. I am none of
those things. Quite often the text about which I have to preach
perplexes me and I would prefer to get out of the job. Often, when
I have to preach about love, I just cannot do it because someone
has been so mean to me that I hate that person and the word "love"
sticks like a bone in my throat. Or else I cannot preach on a subject
because my homelife is upset and disorganized, or because I have
had an argument and every word I say about love shows me up as
a hypocrite. No, I am no letter of Christ because I would have to
be above all that. And yet I am above all that because I trust in
something: I trust that God uses my wretched speech to be the
medium of his presense and that he chooses my speech to be the
vehicle through which he is present. (Dietrich Bonhoeffer said that
the word of the sermon is Christ himself taking and wearing the
human form). Consequently I can take on this letter of Christ only
with the prayer that Jeremiah, knowing his own weakness, prayed
for the Lord's faithfulness: "We acknowledge our wickedness, O
Lord, and the iniquity of our fathers, for we have sinned against
thee. Do not spurn us, for thy name's sake; do not dishonor thy
glorious throne; remember and do not break thy covenant with
us" (Jer. 14:20–21).

I am a credible letter of God only when I do not try to cover up
my own weakness or try to make myself to be more than I am. If
I were to do so I would be just another hypocrite, and hypocrisy
is the very opposite of what is recommended. The person who is
the opposite of what he or she pretends to be does not appeal to
anyone or attract anyone. On the contrary, such a person repels.
A person who is not credible cannot expect to be one from whom
others draw faith. I can be a credible letter only when I do not
hide my deficiencies and reluctance, my weaknesses as an earthen
vessel, my own smallness of faith. By my admission of all this I
truly praise the goodness of the God who does not let me go.

Paul draws an even deeper witness from this imagery of a letter.
He says that this letter is not one which is written with ink on paper
but by the Spirit of God on the heart's flesh; nor is it a matter of

the letter which kills but rather the spirit which makes alive. These words strike us as very strange. What does Paul mean by them? For one thing, the apostle is touching on the usual point of view that Christianity is a strict, higher religious morality that constantly subjects one to the whip of "Thou shalt not." Here that which the gospel bestows is turned into the exact opposite. Whoever is driven by the "thou shalt" is thereby driven in a direction other than the one in which he wants to go by inclination. But God does not want to play the lion tamer, who by whip and chair and pistol forces his animals to do a trick which is so contrary to their nature. But God does want us to be his letters so that he can write his will upon our hearts. Again we must ask what that means.

To do God's will in our heart means to want what God's will is. But how does this spontaneity in which I cooperate come about, this joyfulness which I associate with the will of God and with which I look him in the eye? To be clear about this one has only to read the psalms which catch something of the joy to be had in the law of the Lord. To me that could be masochism and a self-imposed demand only if I overlooked the decisive requirement which makes this praise of the law possible—namely, all the requirements which belong to those who have heard the word of promise with which the Decalogue begins: "I am the Lord your God . . . ." If I experience for a fact that he is my God, that he means so much to me and that he is gracious to me, then I on my part can be open to him and love him. How much more can we Christians love him, we who love him in the form and person of Jesus and experience him here as the one who confers peace and security upon us; as the brother who goes at our side when we must go through the darkness of loneliness, suffering, and dying; who experience him as the one who throws his cross as a bridge across the chasm which separates me from God? God's Spirit gives me this gift of love, and that gift of love makes me a new person and brings about basic changes. Now I no longer have to go over my own corpse (that is what being killed by the letter means). I no longer need to allow myself to be disciplined by the "Thou shalt." Rather, my heart is motivated to will what God wills.

Moreover, the gift of freedom is given to me with this gift of love (2 Cor. 3:17) at the same time. Whoever stands under the pressure of "Thou shalt" is led by the nose. Such a one has to move

on the tracks that have already been laid according to a fixed
schedule and can in no way decide in which direction he will go.
But there is freedom where the Spirit of God enters my heart.
There I become emancipated and am given the right to make my
decisions in a responsible way.

What I am saying all sounds quite general and vague. An example
can clarify what I am trying to say.

In the Sermon on the Mount we read about offering our gift
(Matt. 5:23). As long as I am ruled by the law and am bound by
its letter, I am ordered away from the altar so to speak; I am under
the rule of "religious duty." The people who know me well probably
know that I do not get along with my neighbors and say "Look at
that hypocrite! He mixes everything with a pious babble and fights
with his neighbor all in the same breath."

But if I am a letter of Christ, then I must seek out what I have
to do in a situation. I have to ask myself how I can get out of all
the contradictions. I even have the freedom to close the Bible from
which I derived my edification, put away my hymn and prayer
books, and even stop going to church in order to become reconciled
to the brother with whom I am at odds.

In this kind of freedom I can do all kinds of unusual things
which do not fit into the usual pattern of Christian behavior. God
clothes me with such powers. I am no longer a servant nor a slave.
I am the Master's child and I have the right to say what I consider
right in God's sight. I cannot do that blindfolded, and one need
not fear that I will turn everything upside down. After all, I have
to keep in mind who gave me this freedom. As long as I remember
that I have God's Spirit in my heart and for that reason I will use
my freedom as God would want me to use it, then my freedom is
a disciplined freedom (Rom. 6:1, 15)!

When Paul refers to us as a letter of Christ, he makes a statement
about our true being. Who or what am I in the final analysis?

How many people—especially young people—ask that question!
They do not know who they are or what they are here for. The
quest for their identity makes them uncertain and unhappy. It is
here that we experience that we could be a letter of Christ. This
letter is not a personal description that identifies us but a letter of
pure promise. And it is in the name of these promises that we may

now begin to blossom. Often we may grow faint and even forget the letter and fall back on all kinds of junk mail and advertisements. But this letter is addressed to us personally. God knows our name and he knows where we live. Even if I should forget my own name and identity, he does not. He knows and calls me by my name, for I am not my own, I am his.

CHAPTER 4

What Is a Believing Christian?

Every one who believes that Jesus is the Christ is a child of God, and every one who loves the parent loves the child. By this we know that we love the children of God, when we love God and obey his commandments. For this is the love of God, that we keep his commandments. And his commandments are not burdensome. For whatever is born of God overcomes the world; and this is the victory that overcomes the world, our faith. Who is it that overcomes the world but he who believes that Jesus is the Son of God?

1 John 5:1–5

Our text gives us a very human picture in which we have all the events of the salvation story, albeit only indirectly. And even though the Easter event is not specifically mentioned, this text used to be read as the epistle lesson for the Sunday after Easter. The text presumes faith in Christ, but it does not enlarge on or develop what that faith is. Rather, the text directs our thinking to what faith sets in motion in our lives, to what it is that proceeds from faith. So, then, the theme of this text is the believing Christian.

In our proclamation of the gospel and in our theology, I think we ought not to be frightened off by the question whether this or that be possible, or whether one can make a genuine testimony to what is questioned. My argument is that in all integrity we should be clear about what interests us. Then there can be no doubt that it interests us very much what happens in belief and the believing person. The Bible, for its part, leaves no doubt that God is interested in what comes out of our faith. He plants us in his kingdom and he inquires after the fruits of the tree he has planted.

In asking what comes of faith and how faith develops, I would like to know how someone like Augustine or Bodelschwingh came by his faith, how he overcame doubt and conflict, if faith and life were congenial to each other, or if there were tensions and contradictions. Should the faith of these people have been discernibly manifest? Were these people really credible?

Let us be honest: the first step to faith hardly happens by asking what Christians believe. The first question is resolved inquisitiveness: How does someone live his faith, bear witness to his faith; is his faith worthy of my following? The first question always refers to the witness and not to the testimony he bears. Often that is how people say goodbye to the church. People have concluded that the pastor is not trustworthy (Just look at his private life! He is not interested in the young people! He doesn't care about the old or the sick. He neglects the shut-ins!). The institutional church is not trustworthy. Just look at its bourgeois attitude and at the way its message is fragmented and how unrelated it is to the world. Moreover, in many cases the church does not practice what it preaches.

The first signs of separation from the church are, as a rule, quite personal in nature. One takes offense at those with whom one has dealings, and because the witness gives offense, one is quick to take offense at that to which they bear witness.

I have often thought that this role of the individual does not just hold true when it comes to one's personal relationship to the Christian church. The same thing is true in other areas, for example, among dissidents in Communist countries. They did not turn sour on Marxism because they found fault with Marxist doctrine but because they took offense at individual Marxists and at the contradiction between what they professed and taught and what they actually practiced.

In all of this it is not primarily a matter of the object of faith that is concerned but rather of what people who believe have to say. Or, to put it another way, our text is concerned with the question: How do people understand themselves in the light of Easter? What happens to believing? What effect does faith have on our relationship to our neighbor? Does it unleash any powers of love? How does one who believes meet the demands God imposes in his commandments? How does faith help believers cope with their relationship to the world? Do Christians deport themselves differently, are they different from other people? What is different or special about Christians? Those are interesting questions! For a moment we must not look directly into the "sun of righteousness" himself— that would blind us—but rather we are here called upon to observe the plethora of colors through which this ray of sunlight shines forth.

If we express it this way it is clear that we cannot confine ourselves to describing human circumstances. To put the matter in the terms of Goethe's doctrine of colors: whoever speaks of colors must also speak of the light which lets the colors be seen; he must speak of the struggle of this light with darkness. One can hardly describe anyone who stands in Easter light and has found faith in that light without speaking of this light, indeed, of the very source of light.

Let us begin our thought experiment exactly as our text does, with that person who stands in Easter's light. What is such a person like?

How can we know who is a Christian? In general we know what kind of answer to expect to this question. A Christian is not recognized by his dogma or by his confessional profile but by what proceeds from it, from the fruits that are seen or are not seen. In other words, one is interested in seeing how the Christian practices brotherly love, how he acts toward someone who is indebted to him, what he does with his money and much else. There are two thoughts in our text that set themselves against each other in the attempt to discern the identifying marks of a Christian.

First, in 1 John it is not what we Christians do (e.g., when we love our neighbor) that stands in the foreground but rather why we do it. We do what we do because we are "born of God," because we have our origin in him; we love him for that reason and because our life has been given a new start. So the emphasis lies entirely on the motive of what we do. But when we inquire what is the special mark of a Christian we can find it only in the area of motivation. Only here do we find the roots of what a person really is. If two people do the same thing, what they do is not always the same. Why did the philanthropist endow an orphanage? It is possible he did it just so it would bear his name and enhance his reputation. Does that mean that there is an egotistical motive behind what he has done? If that is the case, then his good deed is disqualified because of a questionable motive. It is also possible that an act which is at first questionable is suddenly seen in a positive light when we discover its upright and selfless motive. The Epistle of John presses the question of what it is that moves and motivates a Christian in an area of everyday life.

Then there is a second matter. At first glance it could seem as though John wanted to say this—being a Christian, a child of God, is something that is expressed in brotherly love—and that is something we can see!

If John were to admonish a congregation in this way today there would be unhappy consequences. John would be imposing a new yoke of the law. Love would become something that is demanded— a Christian act. A Christian does this or that and does not do this or that. One expects that of a Christian. Be nice to each other. Overcome what is between you; patch up your differences. Show the world how full of love you are, that you stand arm in arm together.

If that were what John was calling for, then the same thing would have come of it as came the law of Moses—narrowness and hypocrisy—and beyond this there would be the sense of shame when the law is not kept, that one must continually admit failure.

Perhaps I should explain by an example what I mean when I say the law is unnatural. I once knew a person who quite rightly enjoyed the reputation of being a Christian person, whose otherwise noble character was flawed by legalism. This man was constantly faced with the question: what do people expect of me as a Christian and how can I live up to that expectation? They think, for example (and there is something to it), that a Christian is always ready to serve his Lord and must serve him gladly. So whenever someone expected this acquaintance to do a disagreeable chore he would always respond (with an emphatic tone of voice and look in his eye) with "Gladly." (I can still hear his pious intonation of the word.) But it was galling to him. That, however, dare not be the case with Christians. When his promising and dearly beloved son died in the war he received expressions of sympathy with a beaming smile. Anyone who knew him knew what all this meant. He wanted to bear witness to others that a Christian should not fall into mourning, that in every hardship a Christian should be in control of himself and of good cheer. Still it was clear that he really was not happy in doing this. One sensed something fraudulent about him. Certainly it was not a conscious act of hypocrisy that in this case pretended not to be sour and sad but to be of good cheer (cf. Matt. 6:16) and sought to persuade people that all mourning was overcome. He thought he had to suppress his grief and witness to the strengthening power of his faith to himself and to others.

Here, then, it boiled down to a matter of legalism which tried to force being a Christian. In this way it would be legalistic if we tried to puff up the emotions of brotherly love because these are what a child of God is supposed to feel. John's epistle certainly has nothing to do with this portrayal of what a Christian is like.

The fact is our text strives in an entirely different direction. Here it is not a matter of diagnosing empirical methods of conduct but a promise—or, if you will, a consolation. Do not worry about a Christian program or a set of rules of conduct but trust the evidence: where something like the love of God is experienced on one's own flesh, the love for one's brother comes of itself. It is a spontaneous overflow of love caught up in the experience of God's love.

Theologically speaking that sounds quite plausible and whoever is only slightly acquainted with the problem is familiar with the many arguments which form the basis for this relationship. Yet I must ask myself if it is really all so, if one has not bitten off more than one could chew and if in real life things do not really take a different course. If we observed our own conduct realistically and with alertness, we would find again and again that spontaneity does not happen so simply. Even in particular religious moments of life—for example, when we experience the love of God—we suddenly discover everything else in us as that love toward our neighbor. Even hatred can show itself.

So we see that the love of God and neighbor do not constitute an indivisible whole with us. They are sundered and we fall into a self-contradiction. This is the contradiction Jesus meant—as we have often mentioned—when he uses the word "hypocrisy." Those around us see this hypocrisy sooner that we ourselves. Those around us see our Christian behavior toward our neighbor. So we can understand that those around us see our pious posture for what it is—a religious cosmetic applied over our humanity.

We should not speak all too quickly and dogmatically and glibly about that indivisible context of love of God and neighbor. We have a much weightier problem we can deal with only when we ask—if at all—how such spontaneity of love of neighbor can be.

In light of our text there is a negative answer: this spontaneity is not a certain degree of maturity of the Christian life—like an advanced state of development. The opposite is true. To see this spontaneity take shape I must point to its beginning—back to the reason for its origin. This spontaneity comes about because of the new birth (John 3:3), really through a new beginning, not through progress or perfection. And this new birth takes place when I see Jesus the crucified, risen, and exalted one as my Lord—in other words, when I begin to believe.

If I really understood what happens in this new birth and apply myself to it, then I would really have everything—a new breath of life, distance from petty sorrows and anxieties that beset and trouble me. I would also love my fellow man.

That is what Luther means when he keeps reminding us that we and our thoughts are not judged as to our progress and perfection of our Christian faith but rather should always return to the beginning of our being a Christian, that each day there must be a return to faith's beginnings. We do not grow beyond our baptism; we can only crawl back into it.

Still, I fear that that is all too general and could sound too commonplace. It is so easy to put what is dogmatically correct into words. But what we say is empty if we cannot give a concrete example of what a return to the origin is like. How does such a return take place in our life?

I can conceive of a certain situation. One day I am depressed because the church's conduct sickens me and presents a miserable picture. I have just heard a miserable sermon—one pious cliché after another. Or perhaps I see depressing weakness shown by the church's leadership. Or one sees all kinds of high positions occupied by twits and misguided souls who promote all manner of nonsense with neither embarrassment nor troubled conscience. What, we ask ourselves with no little discouragement, is to become of this "club"? Perhaps someone could come along and calm our upset by reminding us that the church has always had such things and yet has survived them, that such things always have been and will be. I am afraid that such a person is trying to give me some kind of legalistic tranquilizer and is not really dealing with what worries and concerns me.

But let us imagine another someone who has seen our depression. He tells us simply: "But Christ is risen and he rules the world. Why fret so?" How would it be if such a word came at such a moment? Then the vision of the valley of dry bones would be wiped out. I would then be led back to where all comfort begins; where I would not need to fear and hate the weaklings and pests but could feel sorry for them; and where love could begin to blossom. For Christ did not rise up against all these but rather died and rose for all of them.

We need to be reminded of this place of origin over and over again. For even though the place of origin is the one on which everything depends, we keep forgetting it. We forget the one thing that is needful and which sustains us. Our thoughts are constantly occupied and filled with trivia.

That is why this comforting word must be repeated again and again, why there must be preaching and pastoral ministry, for all are acts of repetition of the things which threaten to ruin us. They lead us back to the origin and beginning.

If we rather are veteran and time-tested servants of God, or even professional theologians, then we recognize all these brotherly words. We know them so well that we can say them in our sleep: "My thoughts are not your thoughts"; "Fear not"; "My grace is sufficient for thee"; and many others. We can also cite the theological contexts in which we find these words. "Theoretically" it is all clear to us. But at the crisis moments of life we find over and over again that we do not have the dogmatic knowledge at hand. We probably know from our own experience what it can mean if someone who has less education than we do says in a difficult situation: "But Jesus lives. Why do you worry so much about the church and secularism?

Why do you get so upset?" Theoretically I understand what such a person is saying. I know all that. But here someone reminds me of this lost wisdom. He makes me actualize it. He calls me back to the original locus of my faith.

If we make out of this experience of faith an exercise of our faith of which we consciously take hold, then it has an exceptional meaning for our life. How differently we will then read our newspaper! How much more closely distant people would draw! How differently this earth as a whole—the earth we see under different perspectives on television—appears to us. Even if the earth heaves in convulsions, it is the same earth which once bore the cross of Christ, over which the rainbow of reconciliation shines. But that needs to be said to us over and over again.

I know someone who does this spiritual exercise repeatedly, even when he sits at the wheel of his car. Apart from the city's traffic jams and the bewitching magic of traffic lights there are more pleasant stretches of road! As he drives along these roads he recites his own version of the Gloria Patri: "Glory be to the Father who watches over us . . . to the Son our Lord and brother who walks and drives along with us; and to the Blessed Spirit who wants to fill us and bestow joy upon us; as it was in the beginning, is now and ever shall be world without end." In this way he calls himself back to the point of faith's origin and discovers ever anew beyond the confusion of daily business that peace which passes all understanding.

So we can learn to understand what it could mean when we say that faith is a victory that overcomes the world (1 John 5:4). As the great Bible scholar, Martin Koehler, lay dead in his casket someone said: "He looks just like a disciple." After what has been said let us not misunderstand this remark. It may be that a lifetime of companionship with God ultimately leads to putting behind us all that which oppresses and bedevils us in this world. Shortly before his death the dying Koehler had said: "Now there is nothing that stands between me and God." But even that was only a return of a man who had been a believer all his life to that beginning point where he knew that the Lord had come to him and that faith had laid hold of him. So the dying Koehler looked thankfully back upon the history of his life and faith, the beginning of which he remembered and into which he crept more and more. Our text from John does not intend to look to see such a final goal toward which we look with hope, but rather to look back to what has already happened. Jesus *has* come; he has overcome the anxiety which besets the world (John 16:33). He has ascended and he reigns. Faith overcomes the world not because faith is a stubborn posture over against the world but because it trusts him who has overcome and now is the ruler of all. Faith conquers the world and death because of him of whom we sing

> He lives, he lives, who once was dead
> He lives my everliving head.

To be able to appreciate and understand this we must realize that what is placed before us is finished business. We need to realize that what has happened in the past is valid for today and continues for all eternity. That is what the Epistle of John means when it turns our glance backward to the one from whom all spiritual life flows.

Friedrich August Tholuck has put into verse a little piece of self-examination which may help us find that origin of our faith in everyday life.

> Let every day my question be
> Who rules this heart of mine?
> Do I stand in grace,
> Head toward that place
> Where I am ever thine?

CHAPTER 5

Do Not Be Conformists!

I appeal to you therefore, brethren, by the mercies of God, to present your bodies as a living sacrifice, holy and acceptable to God, which is your spiritual worship. Do not be conformed to this world but be transformed by the renewal of your mind, that you may prove what is the will of God, what is good and acceptable and perfect.

Rom. 12:1–2

Suppose for a moment that we heard these words of Paul for the first time as we sat with a group of people who had been asked to take part in a little psychological test in which each one would tell what had been on his or her mind most of the day. Barring some kind of world upheaval which overshadows all personal matters, we can well imagine what kind of answers such a question would elicit. Certainly all manner of family concern and joys would be mentioned; so would marital and work-related problems. Somewhere along the line there is bound to be someone who has a very close and dear friend or relative who is suffering from cancer. How openly can one speak with such a person about his or her condition? Or should one say nothing at all? Would it not be better simply to remain silent? Perhaps another has problems with a coworker or with the boss. Others are eagerly looking forward to a holiday or a reunion with friends whom one has not seen for a long time.

If we were to look closely at the answers we would receive to the question I have posed we would see how preoccupied people are with the host of the little joys and sorrows that go with everyday living. Certainly it is not saying too much when we say that if God does not mean anything to us in the midst of these everyday concerns, then he does not mean anything to us at all. If that were the case, God would be closed out of all that forms and shapes our lives. It is precisely about this dealing with the routine, the little things of everyday living about which the apostle Paul speaks in our text.

We can deal with this matter on several levels. For example, we can deal with this matter like a father who points an admonishing finger at us and says: "Stop your nonsense and get to work. Manage your time or you will never amount to anything." Or, we can deal with the matter by quoting and reciting proverbs and aphorisms which capture life's deepest experiences in brief and state with directness and an economy of words the fundamental laws of human existence. For example: "A lie has short legs"; "Murder will out"; "Don't count your chickens before they are hatched." Certainly this method is on a higher level than that of the admonishing finger, but it is not the level on which Paul speaks here.

We attain to Paul's level, however, only when we realize that our text is preceded by eleven powerful chapters in which Paul—partly in the style of personal confession and partly in the style of one who is doing some deep and serious theological thinking—declares that since the Christ-event everything is different between God and us. Paul is saying that from that point on we are acceptable to God; there is absolutely nothing, not even a heavily burdened conscience, no torturous problem, which can pluck us out of God's hand and rob us of our peace with him.

That is what the directions for Christian behavior in the last chapter of Romans are about. Nor are they just pious words! The Greek word which Paul uses has a more encompassing sense, that of help for living. The key to this help for living is to be found in the question: What does the certainty that we are accepted by God mean for our lives? What explosive, world-shaking power does this certainty have in our lives?

Paul draws consequences from the basic structure of our faith. He points to these consequences when he speaks of what is usually translated as "reasonable service." Even though this is what the text literally says, this is nonetheless an imprecise translation. What is meant here is far more what God wants of us and what is spoken to us as gospel and direction when God gives assurance of his loving closeness to us (Rom. 12:1). I suppose it would be better to translate "reasonable service" as intelligent, sensible worship.

This summons to sensible worship is a summons for the Christian to do some serious thinking, for a Christian is not someone who simply believes without a second thought—for that matter, without even a first thought. Nor is a Christian an activist who, often hectically, plunges into one social-action cause after another. Rather, the Christian is a reflective person, one who is always concerned with the question of what one does this afternoon or intends to do tomorrow morning has to do with one's faith. The Christian asks: How do I behave when there is discord and quarreling in my family—perhaps with my own children, or my landlord, or my tenant—or in the struggle for status and prestige among my co-workers? How do I behave so that my faith gives me some guidance and does not discredit or cheapen that faith in my own eyes or in the eyes of others?

Anyone who does not think about the relationship between what one believes and one's everyday conduct, and who does not struggle daily with this problem becomes either a hypocrite who indulges in pious self-gratification, or one who, in daily conduct does not want to be troubled with God, or else becomes constantly involved in one goalless pursuit after another. Paul, on the contrary, has in mind the kind of Christian who constantly lives in the world of two words: if . . . then. If God is in fact my God, then, because he is my God, the coworker I encounter every day at the job, the woman I love, my landlady (even though she may be an old bat) is my neighbor.

Let me put it another way. If the gift of faith has been granted to me, that means I become a person who loves. I begin to suffer when I discover that I do not have so much love in me as faith says I ought to have; that I am less than what faith says I should be. Or, to put it yet another way: if God knows what I need before I myself know what I need (Matt. 6:8), then all my worries have lost their sting. It would be inconsistent with my faith to be assailed by these worries. If I nonetheless permit these worries to assail me I am inevitably driven into a corner. On the one hand I believe in God and ground my life in trust in him. But on the other hand, the worries which plague my life involve a lack of confidence in God and cause me to act as though God were not really the Lord of this world.

And so our lives are filled with inconsistencies and contradictions because we cannot come to terms with the business of "if . . . then." That is why it is so characteristic of Paul's directions for living that they begin with the word "test." The Greek word for "test" has a wealth of meanings. For example, the word means simultaneously such activities as to make distinctions, to examine, to differentiate; in any case, it means to reflect and to ponder. My life as the life of one who believes has to be tested repeatedly as to its authenticity. That is the meaning here. Particularly noteworthy is Paul's illustration of this responsibility to reflect and examine oneself: do not make deals with the world. "Do not conform yourselves to this present world." Or, as our modern sociologists would put it, do not be conformists! All of us are inclined to conform, even though we disguise our conformity as nonconformity.

The conformity to the world against which Paul warns us here is not something brought about by the world's use of cruel force, for example, threatening us with the ultimatum: conform or perish. The seduction to conform to the world is by no means so obvious and crude. If that were the case, then any dunce could see through these seductions. No, the seductive temptations are more like those of the serpent in the Garden of Eden. The serpent did not announce its evil intentions to Eve, but pretended sincerely to want to engage in a harmless theological discussion about God. Life is filled with conditional sentences which are dangerously persuasive because they make sense.

If you do not go along with things, *if* you do not parrot the slogans and catch phrases of the day, *then* you are a reactionary. By not going along you are telling the world that you are far behind the times. Who wants to see himself and what he stands for compromised in this way?

Or, *if* you do not go along with all the things that are called progress and progressive, *then* you just have not caught the spirit of the times and are shutting yourself out of the future. You soon will be ready for the scrap heap. In the very moment we turn away from that kind of consequence and keep up with the times—in other words, abandon our critical stance toward the world—we have already conformed to the world; swept under the rug are the questions of what God wants of us (and what he wants of us is probably the opposite of the tendencies of the times), to what kind of future he wants to lead us.

So you see once more we are dealing with a question that demands reflection: we must learn to discern the temptations of the times, and at the same time recognize our weakness for them. Above all, we need to recognize that we must endure repeated attacks of weakness in the face of our yearning for the security of conforming, or, as the sociologists (who have a penchant for giving names) put it, accommodation to the structure. If I may use a contemporary term, I could quite seriously translate Paul as saying "Get emancipated." So what Paul is saying in our text is that God has called you. Examine yourselves and see if you want to conform to God's will. And make no mistake about it; conformity to the spirit of the times resists God's will. You cannot carry water on both shoulders; you cannot simultaneously serve God and man; nor can you serve both time and eternity.

Everyone talks today about changing the structure of society. That is supposed to be the panacea for every problem and ill. But we Christians say that it is rather we ourselves who must be changed. We take seriously this business that God has accepted us and that we have been removed from the dominion of the world to that of God. As a matter of fact, Paul is speaking of a world-shaking change (in Greek the word is *matamorpheirthai*—Rom. 12:12). But this metamorphosis takes place in ourselves as the renewing of the spirit. The initial act in this renewing of the spirit is insight, so one may also call it a thinking event, a reversal in thinking so radical that our existence is no longer determined by the world (so that we just function and perceive the world's sense) but by God, in whose image we have been created. Really, we are emancipated. "Christians are different" we could say, plainly and simply.

The part of our text which deals with our transformation is the injunction to "offer your very selves to him: a living sacrifice. . . ." This strikes us as a peculiar expression and we get at its meaning only when we are clear about what the New Testament means when it speaks of the body. When Paul speaks of the body he means us in our concrete earthly existence. So then, in this existence or body we stand before the decision of whom we will obey; whether this body shall be a temple of the Holy Spirit (1 Cor. 6:19) or a body of whoredom, which is made subservient to an alien power (1 Cor. 6:12ff.).

In order to understand what Paul is talking about we must look more closely at his obvious purpose of clarifying and illustrating what he is talking about by means of the Old Testament practice of animal sacrifice. What is concerned here is not a parallel but a contrast. Two differences assert themselves here between the Old Testament and the New. First, the new worship which Paul has in mind is no longer just a cultic act performed in the temple. Just as Jesus Christ was sacrificed outside the gate (Heb. 13:12), so we must go outside the gate, indeed, out into the world. Paul means here the worship that goes on in the secular, everyday world, not just the worship that takes place in church on Sunday morning. To be sure we have been called out; we have been emancipated. But as those who have been transformed we are sent back to whence we came in order to be the salt of the earth, the light of the world. Even our celebration of the Eucharist would be misunderstood if we took it to be a cultic rite of the original Christian congregation, the rite of the spiritually elite. Like the original observance of the Passover meal, with which the Eucharist is intimately related, the fellowship at the table of the Lord is supposed to be a celebration of decampment, of going forth—whether it be that we, strengthened by this meal, are dismissed to go back to our jobs, our homes, our desks, or, just like sheep, we are sent out among the wolves.

The second difference noted here over against the earlier sacrificial worship may be expressed thusly: to put one's very self at another's disposal. Each of us offers sacrifice in one way or another. But what does that really mean? Almost everywhere one can be represented by someone or something. It does not have to be, as in the case of the Old Testament, a lamb or a fruit of the field. Even our money can function as our representative. The transferral of money from one account to another for some good cause does not disturb or annoy us. Evil tongues often say—and not always without justification—"He (or she) just gave this gift (it is tax deductible, you know) to salve his (or her) conscience." At times these tongues are even less charitable and suggest that such gifts are made simply to win or maintain social prestige. Under these circumstances such gifts are nothing but moral fig leaves. Along the same line, we can substitute participation in demonstrations and quasi-political involvement for exercising our duty to help a sick neighbor who needs our help. When a person of means, for example, who has no personal sense of committment gives me a sum of money for prisoners' welfare, I accept the money with gratitude. But when someone becomes personally involved in the cause to the extent that he or she invites prisoners into his or her home for Christmas, or when an elderly lady on Social Security denies herself to give a few dollars to a worthy cause, then such people are already present with their bodies. One could even say of them that they got involved for God.

So then, Paul calls upon us again and again to think and reflect. What does your sacrifice mean? What do you hope to accomplish by it? We need to think, to contemplate ourselves with a critical eye. To do so is to experience some preludes of the last judgment, at which we shall someday experience what we really were and wanted and did.

The peace of God with which Paul's Letter to the Romans concludes is no cushion on which to rest. Rather it is a height toward which I must stretch. I myself have not yet reached that height. This becomes clearer to me every time I submit this self-examination to the scrutiny of God.

But I am also one who has been laid hold of. A hand has touched me. And regardless how often I have failed, how much despair I suffer, failure and despair cannot harm me. I am called by my name and my name is written in the book of life. That simultaneously becalms and disturbs me; for the peace of God does not lull one into drowsiness and sleep. Rather, God's peace is a mover and shaker without compare. God's peace is the power with which we go forth, outside, before the gate, into the world.

CHAPTER 6

Where Is Abel
Your Brother?

But the Lord God called to the man, and said to him, "Where are you?"

Gen. 3:9

Then the Lord said to Cain, "Where is Abel your brother?"

Gen. 4:9

The word "where" plays an important role in the first pages of the Bible—a role we need to think about. The man Adam had eaten of the forbidden fruit and thereby trespassed upon the majesty of God. Then he hid himself in the bushes when he was overtaken by pangs of a bad conscience. But God searches him out of hiding with his insistent question, "Where are you?" When Cain murdered his brother, Abel, and the blood which was shed cried out to heaven, God put the question to Cain: "Where is Abel your brother?"

There is irony to God's asking where someone is. He is the omniscient one; certainly he knows everything, so he must know where we are, and what is wrong with us. He knows about Adam's and our lostness before we ourselves. He witnessed Cain's heinous act long before the thought had reached fruition, indeed, before the heinous motive took root in Cain's mind.

God does not ask his question just to make small talk. Rather, he asks his question in order to tell something to the one he questions. There is something Socratic about his question: he wants to deliver the person whom he questions of something. The person who is being questioned should be clear about where he stands.

That is how Nathan, the prophet, dealt with David when the king had one of his soldiers—with whose wife David was having an adulterous affair—murdered at the front. Nathan did not preach of censure to David. One can defend himself against a sermon of censure by raising all manner of objections in self-defense. And an intelligent man such as David could certainly raise a number of such objections. That is why it was important to Nathan that David should not assume a defensive posture but should pronounce judgment upon himself. We can pronounce such a judgment as David did only when we do not see our interests being jeopardized, when we see the matter at hand as something that pertains to others, not ourselves. When it concerns others we willingly and enthusiastically apply all manner of critical standards. So Nathan tells the king a touching story about a wealthy herdsman, the owner of a huge flock of sheep, who robs a poor fellow of his single animal, a beloved household pet, with the intent of slaughtering it. When David becomes visibily enraged at such conduct and pronounces his condemnation of the rich man, Nathan looks David squarely in the eye and says: "You are the man" (2 Samuel 12). Thus David has pronounced judgment upon himself. Nathan had made him realize that he and he alone was the guilty party. Thus, through the prophet, God had twice spoken his question "Where?"—David, where are you?" and "Where is your faithful servant Uriah?" God does not simply confront us with "Adam, you are a blasphemer; Cain, you are a murderer." In spite of all the evidence God comes to us with a question and Adam and Cain must answer. They have to come clean and admit what they have done: "I have eaten forbidden fruit"; and "I have shed my brother's blood."

The sequence of the questions is most decisive. What God has to say to Cain hits especially close to home with us moderns. Fratricide is not strange to us. We see it and hear of it every day in the media. I need think only of those ideological dictatorships that intern those who dissent from them in mental institutions and subject them to all kinds of brainwashing, or of all kind of terrorism and racial discord and the like—practiced in the name of religion. And we do not have to look to the far corners of the earth to find examples of such fratricide. All we have to do is to look at our front door to see the victims of fratricide among us, for example, illegal alien workers, those released from penal institutions whom we reject and thereby force into recidivism because they just cannot make a go of life outside a penitentiary.

The question "Where is Abel your brother?" we understand at first as aimed at getting under our skin. Many react to it by deciding to help, probably less by deeds (unfortunately) than through protests and extensive programs. Yet there is something that has been heard.

Still the question is raised: can I really hear and understand what concerns my brother if I have not previously heard the other question, "Adam, where are you yourself?" Only when I am compelled to ask this question about my own whereabouts—I am, after all, Adam!—do I experience the true source of misfortune and the true crisis of my fellow humanity.

Because I am no longer there for God I am no longer there for my neighbor. That is the sequence. If I myself have not experienced the wonder of being accepted—and above all I mean the final acceptance by God himself—then I cannot accept my neighbor. Then I see my fellow man as a competitor or as a partner in a partnership, or as a party comrade, or as one who represents the opposition. But I no longer see in him one who is the apple of God's eye. I no longer see who it is that relates us to each other and who it is who is asking me about my brother, then neither do I hear the question about "Where" (Where are you? Where is your brother?) any more.

So then God's question about the whereabouts of Abel presupposes God's question about us. The question about us is not a strange dialogue of the soul with God; it does not take place in the seclusion of our inner being but rather gets right down to the business of the question of our brother. The relationship between the reflection about the secrets of our faith and about the brotherly act of helping is indeed close. This relationship needs to be closely considered and sought out. We know where the Scylla threatens on the left and the Charybdis on the right; the pious enjoyment of pure credibility on the one side and blind activity on the other. Only he who understands the two questions about "Where" can understand who God is, what he wants to mean to us, and what he wants of us.

CHAPTER 7

Consolation in the Wilderness

And the whole congregation of the people of Israel murmured against Moses and Aaron in the wilderness, and said to them, "Would that we had died by the hand of the Lord in the land of Egypt, when we sat by the fleshpots and ate bread to the full; for you have brought us out into this wilderness to kill this whole assembly with hunger." Then the Lord said to Moses, "Behold, I will rain bread from heaven for you; and the people shall go out and gather a day's portion every day, that I may prove them, whether they will walk in my law or not. On the sixth day when they prepare what they bring in, it will be twice as much as they gather daily." So Moses and Aaron said to all the people of Israel, "At evening you shall know that it was the Lord who brought you out of the land of Egypt, and in the morning you shall see the glory of the Lord, because he has heard your murmurings against the Lord. For what are we, that you murmur against us?" . . . In the evening quails came up and covered the camp; and in the morning dew lay round about the camp. . . . And Moses said to them, "Let no man leave any of it till the morning." . . . And the people of Israel ate the manna forty years, till they came to a habitable land; they ate the manna, till they came to the border of the land of Canaan.

Exod. 16:2–7, 13, 19, 35

Let me confess at the very outset that it is difficult—at least at the first hearing and reading—to get much spiritual or contemporary meaning out of the wilderness story. Whatever we find here we find much more clearly and directly in the New Testament. Why, then, should we concern ourselves with such obscure texts as this when what is really decisive in the gospel is given in much clearer form elsewhere? Perhaps it is just as much of educational value to tackle these obscure and difficult passages as it is such passages whose import is more obvious. It might well be that in such passages we come upon many a gem we did not expect to find. I am led to make this attempt precisely because the very New Testament passage with which we prefer to replace those dealing with the events of the wilderness experience refer to those wilderness events again and again. The Bible reader again and again finds Paul speaking of the manna in the wilderness as the spiritual food which conveys Christ (1 Cor. 10:2). Paul also sees the prototypes of the salvation event which reaches its culmination in Jesus Christ. And in the Gospel of John (6:32–35) the Lord himself sees the manna of the wilderness as the true bread of life. How can we ignore the foreshadows of the Christ-event when we are surrounded by the fullness of his light? So let us try to understand our text as a predictive event and see it in the light of its later fulfillment.

First there is the physical setting, the wilderness in which God's people underwent their trial. That wilderness—to the Bible's way of thinking—was much more than a historical-geographical concept. Rather it is the place of supreme testing. We see the parabolic nature of this experience if we are clear about three things.

First, this wilderness is a totally empty entity. It is totally devoid of every kind of human and natural aid. There is no shade, no oasis, no landmarks, and, of course, no fleshpots. One can well understand that to a starving, travel-sore people the vision of steaming bowls of food would look good even though they were enslaved in Egypt. In the early postwar years when we were starving I came upon my children licking pictures in their mother's cookbooks. Hunger had turned these household books into a fairy tale which suggested all kinds of reveries to them. The wilderness is truly a parable of lostness and hopelessness. The flight into dreams of tomorrow is a real temptation.

Second, the wilderness is a place of surly disgruntlement, the place of trial. To complain means to stir up ill will, to look for a scapegoat. And Moses filled the bill. Is not he the one who caused us to endure all this hunger and thirst? Actually, however, God is the target of these complaints. The griping is aimed at him. The cloud and fiery pillar that led the people did not lead them to very much. They did a terrible job!

Even the way in which the people complained is interesting. The people have the interesting characteristic when they get into difficulty to complain and argue that great burdens have been laid upon them. One of the ways by which they do this is to idealize the past. Compared to those wonderful, good old days the present is a time of darkest misery. Then one can feel sorry for oneself. That the past was filled with slavery and that there was not always the odor of meat and good food on the stove was something they forget. The jam in which one now finds oneself needs the golden background. Even our complaining is similarly penetrating and helps itself to a nostalgic past—the very old yearn for the old days under the kaiser. The young people, on the other hand, choose the enlightened future and measure the circumstances of social injustice and atomic destruction against a utopian "someday." Whether past or present, it is all the same old tune and melody.

We experience similar things over and over in the course of time: we groan under the stress of our work and at the worst moments we flirt with a vision of vacation—we loaf about on a shore somewhere where no one demands anything of us; the sun, sand, and heaven surround us. When such a moment comes—and it often comes suddenly and we can suddenly turn it on—we have the feeling that a great emptiness has overcome us. Suddenly our leisure becomes a wilderness in which we begin to wander and we are caught in the same old pattern.

The contrast between the fleshpots and the wilderness are a part of life. Our fantasy has a remarkable desire to build up such contrasts and to find satisfaction in them.

Even in the life of Jesus the wilderness appears as a place of trail. In the emptiness where all external things and impressions fall away, the spirits of doubt arise. It is the hour when the anti-godly power gets wind of its chances. And this spirit of doubt presses the Lord with the question: Are there not other ways than the cross, painless ways to Christianize the world than on that dreadful instrument of death on Golgotha? Suppose I jumped from the pinnacle of the temple and had angels lower me gently to the ground? Or if I fed the masses with stones that had been turned into bread? Or suppose I allowed the devil to turn over to me the rulership of the world? Would that not have people eating out of my hand, would they not flock to my banner and sing my song if they ate my bread? Why then the way of pain and grief of Golgotha? The emptiness of the wilderness is the place of trial.

Third, at the story of Jesus' temptation, after having rebuked Satan's temptation, we read that angels surrounded and served him. Even the comforts of God have their time when human help is far away and nature withholds its gifts. So the cloud from which God speaks appears over the people. Just as he used to see the arms that were outstretched to him in supplication, he is near at hand in the emptiness of the wilderness. Indeed, when the need is greatest, God is closest!

God provided for his people in the wilderness by miraculous means: quail and manna. But in so doing he makes use of a natural means, for Tamariski shrubs are still to be found there. But here the Hebrews discover that they are fed in the wilderness by a miraculous act of God. The very name of this food reveals in language how a natural event shows God as a helper on the spot—the people, when they notice that the ground is covered with these hardened drops, are filled with astonishment and ask "What is it?." And that is where the question stands. The question is not answered by some biological explanation and given an appropriate name. The word "man(na)" is really nothing more than a rewriting of the question "What is this?" It is a verbal form of astonishment rather than a name, much like the designation "Jahwe" for God. "Jahwe" is not a name that appears along with other names such as Zeus or Wotan. But "Jahwe" too means to cause astonishment, for it says only "I am who and what I am and will be." God did not give his own name and thereby permit himself to be laid hold of when Jacob asked him the question at Jabbok, "What is your name?" (Gen. 32:29). God does not make himself known through names but through blessing activity.

A unique characteristic of manna is that it cannot be preserved from one day to the next. One is immediately reminded of the fourth petition of the Lord's Prayer concerning our daily bread. Even in that prayer we are not talking about a long-term food supply but rather we are reminded to pray each day for each day's bread and to trust for that bread from day to day. That bread is the same as God's word: it wants to be a light which lights our path only from step to step that we may with assurance go our way in the dark. That word is by no means a spotlight that lights the way hundreds of yards ahead so that we can see what lies before us. God's manna provides for each day anew by filling hands and mouths.

One more thing about manna. After five days of daily rations, there was a double ration on the sixth day to provide for the Sabbath. In this case food holds for the coming day. Even under the circumstances of the wilderness the Sabbath rest is proclaimed. Here we probably have one of the oldest reports about the Sabbath commandment. Certainly it is worth thinking about that this commandment should turn up in the terror of the wilderness experience. The modern, practically minded, ecumenical balance between activity and relaxation, between the current output and the reloading of the adding machine is not of concern here. There is something else. Whoever takes this commandment about the day of rest and worship seriously and obeys it can rest assured that God will provide for it. In modern speech we would say he who closes down on Sunday morning in the name of God and because he wants to and leaves his desk full of unfinished work, or abandons the harvest which absolutely must be brought in, should be sure that God will keep his promises.

Nor does it concern any calculation about how the wilderness period can best be survived or how regenerative periods of relaxation can be turned on. No—it is rather about a message of trust; the same trust as about the daily bread which we should not think about without trust.

In this text, then, we come across some passages which touch on salvatory happenings which connect Old and New Testaments together.

It is precisely where total solitude prevails that God is present with his aid. He prefers to dwell in darkness and emptiness (cf. 1 Kings 8:12), but he also wants to brighten that darkness and fill the emptiness with his presence. So we find Christ closest at hand with his aid in the upheaval of waves (Matt. 14:24–33) and in the darkness of Golgotha where one cannot see one's own hand in front of one's face much less the hand of God; it is there that we see the dawn of salvation and the turning point of the world.

Further, in the wilderness there are no maps, no planned marches over paved roads. In that wilderness one can go his way only from day to day, like a child seeking its way in a dark and empty place. Yet even in the Valley of the shadow we still possess the rod and staff of the Good Shepherd; we find bridges across the gulleys, comfort in terror and anxiety, nourishment for our hunger.

So one can still sense that here we are reading an ancient code that shows us how God is acting like a red flag that waves for recognition to show all God's saving acts where we trust that he is at work. And his presence is closest where our trust in false gods, and men, and in good luck has turned to naught, where there is absolutely nothing else in which we can trust.

PART TWO

GOD IN AND ABOVE
THE AGES

CHAPTER 8

Eye to Eye with Patriarchs and Prophets

Peter concluded his Pentecost sermon with these words:

"'Let all the house of Israel therefore know assuredly that God has made him both Lord and Christ, this Jesus whom you crucified.'

"Now when they heard this they were cut to the heart, and said to Peter and the rest of the apostles, 'Brethren, what shall we do?' And Peter said to them, 'Repent, and be baptized every one of you in the name of Jesus Christ for the forgiveness of your sins; and you shall receive the gift of the Holy Spirit. For the promise is to you and to your children and to all that are far off, every one whom the Lord our God calls to him.' And he testified with many other words and exhorted them, saying, 'Save yourselves from this crooked generation.' So those who received his word were baptized, and there were added that day about three thousand souls. And they devoted themselves to the apostles' teaching and fellowship, to the breaking of bread and the prayers."

Acts 2:36–42

When someone makes a speech it goes without saying that the speaker is interested in what he is saying.

In itself it is a miracle of the Holy Spirit that it was Peter who preached the Pentecost sermon. Was it not he who had denied the Lord in a critical hour? How is it, then, that a fellow such as Peter delivers the major address on this occasion, that he should speak the praises of the victorious and risen Lord when he had turned

away from him, written him off as a "loser," and denied his own
Christian faith? Whoever heard of someone being a spokesman of
a conviction, of a group of persuaded people—in this case a spokesman of Jesus' disciples—who had turned aside, who had allowed
the banner he once had borne to fall to the ground, recanting his
renunciation and becoming once more a spokesman of him whom
he had deserted?

Such a turnabout can only signify something like a raising from
the dead, a life-giving miracle of the Holy Spirit! Peter does not
speak in his own name—after all, he has been compromised. It is
another who has filled his dead heart with a spirit one recognizes
henceforth as the Spirit of God and not of the man called Peter.
He was, so to speak, approved by the risen Lord himself. If that
had not been the case there would have been a howl of protests
from the ranks of the faithful demanding to know, "How come
this fellow has so much to say when he turned traitor and deserted
his colors?"

How could the Spirit have worked on Peter and brought him to
the way?

Peter preached a sermon on the history of salvation of the Old
Covenant, with which all present were familiar from their childhood. Many familiar names were mentioned among them, David
the king, the prophet Joel, and many others to name just a few of
them. Why does he recite these old and familiar names? It is a
wonder that people did not tap their heads and mutter "the same
old stuff." But Peter's hearers were touched to the quick. Why?
What had happened?

Actually Peter had told an old story, yet somehow that story
conveyed much that was new and full of surprises. What amazed
Peter's auditors most was the experience that in every act of salvation all kinds of lines became evident which pointed to this very
Pentecostal day of this outpouring of the Spirit and the presence
of the risen Lord. Then the old texts suddenly received new life.
These stories laid hold of their hearers who suddenly felt that the
old patriarchs and prophets were standing at their side and that the
past had become the present. There was a kind of simultaneity with
that present. Put rather jovially one could say it was as if a coin had
suddenly fallen; one of those moments of which we say, "Aha!"

To be sure the listeners had indeed heard those old scriptures, and yet they did not know them. Peter had the key that locked them up. And now these scriptures uncovered the secrets that people had unknowingly carried around with them. It was as if people until then had had the Word of God only in a secret code and now, all of a sudden, they read that Word in decoded form for the first time.

We ourselves can have the same experience. For example, we learned the Twenty-third Psalm by heart as children and yet we did not understand it, for life had not shown us those "valleys of the shadow of death" filled with anxiety and lostness reaching for us and where the comforting voice and leading hand and the rod and staff would have some meaning. Only much later, when we stand lost in the rain and are overwhelmed in a situation of complete terror, do these words come to mind with a warmth and understanding that was no longer like so much baggage in the closet of our memory.

We have something of that experience with church windows. We tour a famous cathedral and walk around the outside of the edifice in order to let the architectural proportions have their effect upon us. The fabled glass windows are silent. They are shrouded in gray and have their effect upon us only as constitutive elements of the building. Only when we enter the interior of the building do these windows begin to lay hold of us and speak their message. Then we stand before the figures and events of the history of salvation and, surrounded by its figures and symbols, these figures and events behold us. When the spirit of Pentecost lays hold of someone that person is transported to the inner sanctuary, scales fall from his eyes and he hears something speak which hitherto was silent. The disciples experienced something of Pentecost on the road to Emmaus (Luke 24:13–35). While they were still under the shock of the Good Friday event they were on the road to Emmaus where they encountered their risen Lord. But they did not recognize him. This unrecognized companion who accidentally crossed their path touched on that which Peter, in his great Pentecost sermon had made into a program. Peter revealed and interpreted to his auditors the salvation history of the Old Covenant and showed them that Moses and the prophets had already come and pointed out that which pointed to Golgotha and that what had seemed to them to be a catastrophe had been provided for in God's plan of salvation. What threatened to destroy or interfere with the whole concept of the divine guidance of history was rooted in this idea. Was not Christ supposed to suffer all these things in order to enter into his glory (Luke 24:26)? That was the tone in which the unknown spoke to them and in which the higher-goal-directed thought pointed, which was far above the supposedly accidental and catastrophic happenings of Golgotha. So the disciples of Emmaus came to an "Aha" experience, to a preview of Pentecost. Only after the stranger departed from them did they say to each other, "Did not our hearts burn within us while he talked to us on the roads, while he opened to us the scriptures?" (Luke 24:32). The Geiger counters of their hearts had struck; they sensed an unknown enlightenment. But they did not recognize him who had spoken to them. Above all, where this revelation is given, where these ancient words suddenly become alive and contemporary, the Holy Spirit is at work. We ourselves cannot break open this seal. We stand like bulls at a new gate. We ourselves do not understand Jesus' parables even though they use the most familiar pedagogical illustrative material, the kind that should be clear to every child. But our human spirit is so concerned with our own affairs, our daily hopes and cares, that it cannot break the circle. Precisely there where God comes closest to us and appears to us in the parable in familiar pictures is where we are most aware of our alienation from God. God has to come to our aid with his Spirit and aids us to know who he is and what his Word means. And he does that precisely by the act of breaking out of the circle of human taciturnity. The Bible calls that an act of the Holy Spirit!

This Spirit of God that reveals his secret is always at work. It was the Spirit who opened the eyes of the prophets so that they could say great things. And it was that Spirit who laid hold of the disciples at Emmaus. That at which only hints were given before is now revealed in the Pentecost event. The storm that up to now sounded but slightly has become a primeval storm. From its crater pour forth flames which brighten the night so that the entire world seems changed by its rays. When God's very Word suddenly seems different than before then the world, our life, indeed everyone around me is seen in a different light. This radical transformation of all things and values is more radical than words can describe.

How has the Word of God, the light of the world, become different? Jeremiah points to this transformation in the Old Testament. Let me show what I mean in just a couple of sentences. We speak of dogma as that which must be believed. So in Israel the law was experienced as a compulsion from which one sought to be free. The history of Israel is the story of the attempts to be free of that compulsion. In the face of this great contradiction Jeremiah leads us to the great promises that point to the great revolutionary event of Pentecost. The Lord says he will write his law on our hearts and minds and no one will teach another and say "Know the Lord." On the contrary, says the Lord, they will all know me, both great and small (Jer. 31:33). And in Ezekiel we read in a similar vein that the Lord will give us a new heart and spirit, a heart of flesh that will obey his commandments (Ezekiel 11:19).

What is promised here is this—the Spirit of God transforms the "You shall" of the law's hard stone that is imposed upon us from without and against which we beat our heads into something that is written upon our hearts, so that we no longer stand in opposition to God but are open to him, spontaneously and from the heart. The Spirit of God sees to it that the divine will becomes our will.

That means two things. First, his spirit permeates us so completely that we are filled. Second, there is no contradiction between what God wants and what I want. As Luther puts it, we conform to God and that has consequences that can only be hinted at here. In the modern consciousness that, ethically speaking, has been shaped largely by Kant, the laws of God appear to be a foreign law which can hardly be in harmony with the autonomy of a human being come of age.

Here the distinction between heteronomy and autonomy has been overcome. The Spirit has won a bridgehead on the territory of the I; he has transformed the I so that of itself it is possible to will what God wills.

If we examine more closely the working of the Spirit described by our text we shall make an astonishing observation.

I said that the Spirit of God makes us acquainted with his Word and brings it home, makes it clear to us. The Spirit also does in us what we try to do when we, with our weak and inadequate ability, try to make our message understandable. But if that really happens and we really receive the assistance of the Holy Spirit, what happens then? Do the people nod their heads in an applauding fashion as if to say "fine" or "I understand, thank you"? Have they then tucked it in their pockets?

No. What happens is something entirely different. If on Easter Day we speak the conventional greeting "Christ is risen" then we are just nodding our rather sleepy heads. We are just saying the old familiar—all too familiar—words. Indeed, that is what we have come to do—to declare what we have already known. But when it quite suddenly occurs to us what that means that Christ is risen—in other words we have an "aha" experience and we are shaken out of the familiar and have to change our lives—that is another matter! Then we come to a parting of the ways. Some accept that it is an emancipating word. They throw off the chains of the old life and breathe the air of hitherto-unknown freedom. Others reject it emphatically. They do not want anything that gets under their skin and goes to the heart. They want to remain masters of their own hearts and regard God as a foreign-occupation power on their territory.

That is always the case where the Spirit of God unveils the message of life: this message becomes one both of gospel and judgment. It confronts us with the necessity of making decisions that accept the gift of the Spirit and those that say "Don't bother me." Little wonder that the first critics on that first Pentecost accused those touched by the Spirit of being intoxicated.

In order to clarify and strengthen the meaning of that effect Luther often quoted Isaiah's comment that God's Word will not return void when it is proclaimed (Isa. 55:11). That Word does not inflate itself as a word that is not understood or as a rejected word full of sound that blows away but is always a word that accomplishes something: it accomplishes either faith or rejection.

In either case the Word does not return void, be it loaded with souls won or with souls now compelled to speak their rejection openly. Or, to use a modern term, the ungodly is called out of its incubation and becomes virulent.

Both those who are won to faith and those who reject its call sit

in the same pew in the temple and stand side by side as they listen
to Peter's sermon. The Spirit goes among them and separates one
from the other—something Jesus portrays when he tells of two
men walking in the same field and one is chosen while the other
is rejected. Two will be grinding at the same mill and one will be
taken and the other rejected (Matt. 24:21).

So then Pentecost is the festival of the imparting of the Spirit,
not simply a festival of a highly emotional moment portrayed in
tongues of fire. Pentecost can just as well portray the hour of
judgment on judgment day. Pentecost can portray those alienated
from God and God as a stranger to us. What the Spirit reveals to
us in Pentecost simply does not permit us those pious and romantic
fantasies about a loving father above the starry sky who plucks the
most lyrical strings of our hearts. And it is just this honesty with
which he confronts us in the Pentecost wonder that brings with it
a terror. It is quite different from that pipe-dream vision we used
to conjure up for ourselves.

This happening of judgment, which is worked in out of the
background of Pentecost, can be made clear to us by the text from
Joel (2:30) that Peter quoted which speaks of blood and fire and
smoke so that the sun will turn into darkness and the moon into
blood. In the event of the Spirit God is revealed as the majesty
before whose judgment we cannot stand. Here the terror of God
is at work not in the figure of a nonentity that wraps itself in his
light but quakes as the experience of the end of the cosmos under
his judgments. Yet in the midst of this ballad of destruction and
nothingness there sounds forth the word of comfort and restora-
tion: "It shall come to pass that whoever calls upon the name of
the Lord shall be saved and everlasting arms shall enfold him when
the fragile values of this world and its houses built on sand collapse
and fall."

It is a judgment over those who did not carry the Savior among
them and who together with their children were willing to be guilty
of his blood. At the same time the cross is the bridge that spans
the abyss between God and man. What comes close to people then
is that they cannot continue to live as they have hitherto.

After the rotting fundamentals of existence are broken and transferred to new soil they must establish a new life. This new life must draw its direction and order and style from that which it has experienced. That is why this new life is surrounded by the frightening question: "What shall we do? How shall we live from these stumps?"

People do not ask, "What shall we do to find salvation?" It has just become clear to them that that is a foolish question. One cannot want to achieve that salvation, for God bestows not only the completion but the desiring of it (Phil. 2:13). No. The question is, How can we live in the name of a salvation that has already been granted to us?

Here we see the distinction between repentance in John the Baptist and what the word "repentance" can mean after the great deed of awakening. People at the Jordan River heard John's thundering revival sermon and asked, "What must we do to be saved?" They were told, "He who has two coats, let him share with him who has none." Let even the soldiers and tax collectors receive their wages (Luke 3:11–14). All of that is under the threat of the changing of the age. Repentance here is something like an ethical acid bath with which one prepares for the arrival of him who baptizes with fire and the Spirit. Now the whole world has been turned upside down. That is why everything is turned around. The baptism with fire and the Spirit has already taken place. In the coming of Jesus God has already worked our salvation. All grace has been poured out over us and we ask what consequences this must have for our lives.

Here we see the difference between repentance and all of the dismal things one used to associate with that word. Here the word does not just mean a demand, it is a consequence which makes us ask how we can so order our lives that they correspond to the brightness by which they have been filled. We must no longer have those dark and dusty corners we used to sweep under the rug. The gospel's day penetrates into every nook and cranny: in our family, our relationship to our friends and competitors, in matters of business, money, and sex. Unredeemed spots in our lives not yet touched by the new torture us by their contradiction to the Light. What has not been swept out can undermine our faith.

So get rid of the old patches and vacuum cleaners! It is not a matter of fixing up and repairing our lives here and there, but rather of a new birth worked in us by the Spirit (John 3:3). It is a matter of a new beginning. That is the answer to the question "What must we do?"

We can only go on living when we have experienced this over-powering new experience. It is only the first installment of what will be given to us (2 Cor. 1:22; Eph. 1:14) when God has completed his glorious work, when at the end of the world he will be all in all. It cannot be otherwise—this expectation that God will be victorious and that everything that opposes him will be swept away simply has to find expression in our lives. Pascal once said that it is a joy to be in a storm-tossed boat if one is certain that the boat will not go under. The persecutions which the church is undergoing (not to mention the hardships and injustices we all suffer) are like this. To repent now means to follow this advice and so to conduct ourselves that we make it credible (not only to others but most of all to ourselves) that our ship is coming home. Christ is at the end of the journey and he is the victor to whom the journey leads; he is the Lord who commands the waves and storms.

How do we reach such a point? We do not need a long list of moral rules or exercises. Everything depends on how we enter into the Holy of Holies in which the light-flooded windows proclaim to us the great deeds of God. If we submit to such rules and allow ourselves to be ruled by what is outside ourselves, our life will of itself take on a new shape. That must have consequence when we once more step into the light of day and have to deal with men and circumstances.

This, then, is how Peter answers the question of "What shall we do?" He gives us a very simple answer: "Be baptized and receive the forgiveness of sins, be freed from the past and give room to the Spirit of God." In thought he might add: If you can do that everything will come of itself. Or you might say with Luther: the stone that lies in sunshine will become warm by itself; in other words there is no need to command more. It is an automatic process. Be led through your baptism to the church of God and become members of the Lord's body, trust the promises conferred upon the fellowship with which it is blessed; rejoice in the sustaining strength of this assembly of brothers and sisters and then you will experience the breath of the new life; then you are the brightness and joy and you are rid of the false standards and directions of this lost generation. Then you can face the future with assurance and confidence because you are sure of eternity. Whoever is certain of whom the last hour belongs to need not fear for the next few minutes.

CHAPTER 9

God's Narrow Gate
to the World

Judas (not Iscariot) said to him, "Lord, how is it that you will manifest yourself to us, and not to the world?" Jesus answered him, "If a man loves me, he will keep my word, and my Father will love him, and we will come to him and make our home with him. He who does not love me does not keep my words; and the word which you hear is not mine but the Father's who sent me.

"These things I have spoken to you while I am still with you. But the Counselor, the Holy Spirit, whom the Father will send in my name, he will teach you all things, and bring to your remembrance all that I have said to you. Peace I leave with you; my peace I give to you; not as the world gives do I give to you. Let not your hearts be troubled, neither let them be afraid. You heard me say to you, 'I go away, and I will come to you.' If you loved me, you would have rejoiced, because I go to the Father; for the Father is greater than I. And now I have told you before it takes place, so that when it does take place, you may believe. I will no longer talk much with you, for the ruler of this world is coming. He has no power over me; but I do as the Father has commanded me, so that the world may know that I love the Father. Rise, let us go hence."

John 14:22–31

The disciples to whom Jesus is speaking are anxious and uncertain about what will happen if he leaves them and is no longer in their midst. That puts them in the same situation with us who live in that dreaded in-between time of Jesus' departure and his coming again. It is the time when the prince of this world seems to have a monopoly and mixes everything together—light and darkness—into a twilight and befogs our view so that we no longer can see God's direction. Jesus announces this fellow's ascent to power by saying he is already taking over. It is as if he were saying that there is a super-personal power behind the scenes that seeks to draw us into its field of force. That power has no power over him. It bounces off of him. Yet it is a threat to those who belong to Jesus and those who stand on the field of battle between God and Satan. They must make up their minds on which side they belong. Only when they can believe are they able to resist and can be delivered from the power of darkness. This faith is difficult if the Lord is no longer among them and if his shield no longer stands at their front lighting their way. How shall they withstand the valley of the shadow?

It is simultaneously the time when God threatens to disappear from their sight and in fact does disappear from their view. In any case it seems as though Leon Bloys was right when he said "God is withdrawing from things," that he is giving the prince of this world a free hand. The "will to power" seems to rule in this age, like blind chance rules a plane crash or a natural catastrophe; terrorists go about their business; criminals are seduced by powers that have been robbed of their powers of discretion. One could go on and on giving illustrations that the world is ruled by hands other than God's and that the disciples' anxiety is ours as well. It is to such a time as this that the promises of our text apply.

With Bloys's remark that God is withdrawing from the scene let us listen to the question of Judas Thaddeus: "Lord, why do you not reveal yourself openly to the world?" It is always those who have experienced Christ and want to stay on his trail, as it were, who are most painfully aware of this absence of an open verification.

Suppose for a moment we had been at a gathering of Christian people—any kind of gathering such as a synod convention, a worship service, a dinner. And suppose we had witnessed a powerful proclamation of the gospel and gotten an idea of what the Holy

Spirit can do in such a way that something overwhelmingly new was thrust into our lives. It would become suddenly clear to us that the world had undergone a change, that nothing could remain as it had been if people opened their hearts to this Spirit, if management and labor, journalists and artists were laid hold of by the Spirit and had received a radically new outlook on life.

So we have heard the rushing of the wind for a moment in our ears and seen the Pentecostal flames dance about which consume the old and are simultaneously the signal for a new way. Then we go out to the street filled with the spirit of what we have just experienced; we see people coming from or going to a party, home from work, or staring tiredly ahead or skimming through a tabloid as they sit on the trolley. They are filled with something, even an emptiness, all have something on their minds, all are striving for a goal, each is driven by something—not just by what fills me to the point of frustration and confronts me as a question of fate.

It seems incomprehensible to me that the others are not stirred so that it does not seem to exist for them. Why does it occur only to me, to us? Why does God let people vegetate in their mindlessness? We cannot understand this apathy. But why must this secret barrier develop between them and me? I can feel sorry for these people. But why is this miserable business tolerated? It is like a cold shower for a burning faith.

In a similar way Judas likes to fool around with the disappointment he experienced waiting for the Messiah. Even there everyone should feel something in one's person. The Messiah should be an enormous public appearance and must so intervene with the spokes of the world's wheel that he must astonish everyone. But this whole Messiah effect is not there.

This disappointment is not strange to us. We catch ourselves thinking: how wonderful it would be, the great leaders of the world would recognize Jesus if he were to sit down in their midst.

I remember, during the days of the Third Reich, what an electrifying effect the news had on us that the leader of the Moral Rearmament Movement had gotten access to Heinrich Himmler, the leader of the SS, through Frau Himmler and that the Nazi leader was about to convert. Was it possible that the Spirit of God could penetrate even Himmler's heart of stone? And what a freedom from dreadful pressure it would be if the Spirit could lay hold of this leading figure of Nazi rule, heal the ulcers of society, or fill the makers of public opinion and bring them on a new path. How different everything would become!

Jesus, however, contents himself with the backyards and alleys of the world and disdains the great public places. He avoids the strategically important points from which the world fishes and holds to individuals and people without influence who live on the edges of society—a much-plagued old woman, a cripple, a blind man, a gout victim cause him more concern than Herod or the Roman governor, Pontius Pilate. He inclines his ear to the cries of the powerless and the underdog and does not seek to win audiences with the circles of the great.

Why does he do that? What harm could come of it if Jesus made himself publicly known by jumping from the pinnacle of the temple and were borne to earth by angels so that thousands of onlookers would be influenced by this miraculous legitimation and applaud his godly power, as the Tempter once suggested to him in the wilderness temptation?

In that case he would have appealed only to the exterior garb of people's nerves. In the circus high-diver's act we see how, when the drums of the orchestra become silent, everyone begins to breathe in a synchronized fashion or to hold his breath, be he Christian or atheist, communist or conservative, Catholic or Protestant, child or senior citizen. The beliefs and interests of the circus spectators are otherwise varied. There is hardly anything that unites them and there is no cross-communication among them. The only thing that binds this crowd together and gives it its identity and remains constant is its nerves and reactions. For a single moment there is something that influences all alike.

But when the music starts up again and when the spectators have left the circus, they become again a colorful crowd of people who have nothing to do with each other and who are bound together by nothing. Even the high dive lies an hour behind them when they get home and find an unexpected bill or get into an argument with a member of the family.

The nerves just form the outer layer of our psyche. What puts them on edge does not touch our deepest level. Nerve impressions are limited to split-second punctuality. They are quickly turned about into nothing. The nerves were—and probably still are—the quickest way to reach the public. That is why advertising aims as it does at the nerves rather than at the insight and in this way tries—through sounds and rhythm—to deal with desire and receptivity.

Is that why Jesus rejected the idea of appealing to the sense of the masses by jumping from the pinnacle of the temple? He wanted to win man's heart, man's personal center, and make it his dwelling. He knew that this was the only way to make new creatures of people, and so he did not content himself with impressing people in a peripheral way. He wants our hearts, not our nerves. The heart is the key to his lordship of our lives.

But he realizes there are limitations to his revealing himself. For heart and conscience—the things that concern him—are not the same with everyone. They react differently to him. He will win only a few of them, for the appeal to the heart and conscience compel decision and change. Only a few—a tiny flock—will go the narrow way. The leap from the pinnacle of the temple with its momentary impact would not accomplish his ends, it would only conceal rather than reveal his ends. And Jesus does not want to conceal or misrepresent his gospel.

Were there not other ways by which Jesus could make himself known, ways that would be less questionable than this business with the nerves? A much more serious and far more widely recognized way would be that certain principles of his message would be recognized as the common-sense possession of the common culture. To these common principles could belong the understanding of Christian love which is the readiness born of it to be a human being, to which could also belong the unburdening of sorrow and anxiety. Finally, to this common intellectual possession that could be sure of a general acceptance could belong what we call Christian humanism.

But here there is great objection. Of what good would a social program and culture be without the intimate zone of discipleship, personal faith, without the total engagement of our inner selves.

I remember having had a conversation with one of our leading cultural critics to whom we owe the sharpest analyses of our present situation. He spoke to me of the decisive need about which he was not entirely clear, which had cast its shadow over that evening's lecture, and which had made quite an impression on us. It seemed to him that, contrary to earlier times in his life when he had to deal with anti-Christian effects or ideas, he seemed to become clear in his mind that Christianity was really a reservoir for all values of Western culture. Yet he could not believe, although he had yearned and struggled for the ability to believe after the upheaval of his values and convictions. He had the feeling that his observations only touched the surface but did not go to the heart of things. He could not rid himself of the feeling that it is useless to want to preserve certain values if the basis of these values, their source, is hidden. In short, Jesus of Nazareth for him is the figure who laid the last foundations of our culture, but he can win no personal relationship to him. He cannot call Jesus his Lord because he just does not have that kind of faith. Yet ultimately everything depends on this personal access to him.

I am not at liberty to say what course our conversation took from this point on, or about the reply I gave him. I simply mention these fragments of a conversation because my friend unknowingly had felt and touched upon that with which our text deals: that Jesus turns away from the question of public acknowledgment before the world and concentrates on the matter of discipleship (John 14:23).

Above all else discipleship means to love Jesus and to be lovingly devoted to him. Only when I love him is his word as well as his call to discipleship no longer a law or command to which I must conform—willingly or not—but rather is something that goes to my heart and drives me out of myself to follow him. The old saying of Ezekiel is fulfilled that God will give us a new heart and a new spirit and make us a people that will walk in his commandments (Ezekiel 36:26).

Where the Spirit of God holds sway, there is freedom. To stand in freedom before God means to be no longer cowed by a "You shall not" mentality but to want what God wants and wills. No, it is no longer a mater of "obey my word" but "if you love me and entrust yourselves to me you need no longer obey my word as though you were obeying a command but this word will give you the power to keep it." This Word will drive us to him and our obedience will come of itself. Only one who loves so truly is driven by his Word.

This is why this is really the act of God, his Pentecostal chief deed of inciting the heart is such that we can love. It is happiness and fulfillment to be in harmony with God; it is no longer a sacrifice.

When one understands these circumstances it is quite easy to see why Christ cannot make himself known in any tangible way, nor can we. The church cannot be an agency for propaganda. Christ can enter the world only by way of the narrow gate of a loving heart. That is the reason why there is no Christian ideology with which the world can be indoctrinated. Again and again—especially in spiritually rocky soil, ground that is clearly apathetic—Christian-minded people come up with all kinds of offbeat ideas and experiments. They recommend all manner of humanitarian ideals and portray Christ as the strength that can lead to the realization of these ideals. But these Christian programs for the betterment of human society fade away into the blue and just do not win many followers. People probably say, why should we swallow things just because they are wrapped in Christian wrapping paper? We can get these ideals more cheaply at the ideological marketplaces of the world—from more experienced peddlers. None of these programs can work because everything depends on the relationship to a person. Whoever draws close to that person—lovingly so—his words would pass into flesh and blood. He who is freed for this love is driven to discipleship. Whoever does not draw near to Christ remains a stranger to Christian principles, or else he buys those principles from other outlets.

So it is that the most characteristic Christian assertion is that Christ wants to take up his dwelling place with those who love him, and that dwelling place is the heart. It is from the heart that Jesus wants to take hold of me and lead me by the hand. But he cannot be only a subrenter. If we make him only a subrenter that means we give up only that space which we rarely use. When Jesus speaks of taking up his dwelling he means he wants every room of our house. He whom we say we love does not want to be a burdensome guest who is really welcome only under certain circumstances. On the contrary, he wants to be, and be wanted, where we really are at home.

There are other promises connected with this new spirit in our hearts. The Spirit of God reaches into our future and even makes our past new.

Under his influence our relationship to the future is changed. The concern and fear that formerly prevailed in our relationship are driven off. Even the lights of the false hopes that we once followed so eagerly and hopefully, on which we counted so heavily—these are all snuffed out: "Let not your hearts be troubled." We have a comforter to stand by us. He promises with these words the kind of peace that takes away all anxiety, the kind of peace that knows no terror or fear, no depression or despair.

Peace! How significant that word is in contrast to anxiety! Perhaps we would expect courage or bravery, but peace is another term for what I called harmony with God.

An example from the Middle Ages helps us to understand this word "peace" as the opposite pole to the powers of terror. In those days there was a disease peculiar to monks which was known in religious circles as "akedia." The illness had this peculiarity: people noticed that many monks tended to show signs of anxiety, melancholy, and depression. Diagnosis showed that monks suffering this illness had divided hearts (akedia, literally "neglect"). Although the monks had dedicated their lives to God, their hearts were not entirely in it. Their thoughts and mental states were concerned with things quite contrary to their spiritual service. Their loyalty was divided. And that caused a heaviness of heart, sorrow. To be sure it did not afflict all, but the ailment beset a great many. We see the same illness in many who are not monks. Because we do not trust ourselves to the Lord—that is, love him enough—but still hold on to other things, our hearts are divided. That is a kind of peace that leads to all kinds of neuroses. For this reason halfhearted and lukewarm Christians are even more afflicted than are outright atheists, nihilists, and others who in their own way are one-sided but do not suffer from this division. Troubled Christians often envy these; they do not know what their problem is.

The Spirit of God wants to take all this away from us; God's Spirit wants to show us the other side of the coin. When we give

God's Spirit entrance into our hearts he takes away from us the division of our loyalties. (When I was a boy and misbehaved my mother used to say I wanted so much I did not know what I wanted. So is the human heart divided.)

Whoever receives the spirit of love overcomes the division between what one wants and what one ought to do. That is what peace means.

If I continually say "Thy will be done," then that cannot possibly mean that I really want this and I want that but yet I conform to the higher will of God because one cannot stand up against him. The will to which I submit here is not a personalizing circumspection of fate but the will of him whom I love, by whom I am moved, to whom I want to entrust myself. I am at peace with him and so I can entrust myself to him.

But the Spirit draws me backward to new perspectives of the past. Under the Spirit's influence, what Jesus said and did in the years A.D. 1–30 comes alive among us. "The Holy Spirit will reveal all mysteries and call to mind all that I have said to you." What we did not understand when we first heart it (e.g., in confirmation class), what we have learned by heart begins to take on meaning for us. What in time was just a vivid illustration—for example, the parable of the Lilies of the Field or the Good Shepherd—unleashes its comforts and is laid hold of. When we have troubles we suddenly understand the message of the birds for whom God cares. And when we have to go through the valley of the shadow we suddenly experience and feel the rod and the staff of the Good Shepherd in our hand. We are no longer alone. We have not lost what was once said to us. What was once said to us has not left us but is still there and becomes part of our present and leads us. It becomes the shade under the wings that bring us to peace.

We recognize the biblical image of the wide path that leads to destruction and of the straight and narrow gate that leads to life (Matt. 7:13). What is true of the two ways we travel in life is also true of God's path to us. God does not travel the grand avenues and boulevards which are decorated for the entrance of the great and powerful of this world. No heralds announce his coming. To the contrary! God finds his way to us over the side streets, the back streets and alleys; over weed-covered, trash-strewn paths and via our hearts into the world. He needs men who put themselves at his disposal and permit him to take up his dwelling in their hearts. Only via our inner life can God come to us.

Sodom needed only ten righteous men to save that part of the world (Gen. 18:32)! Could it be that only ten hearts that are unconditionally opened to love, that offer God a home, are all that is necessary for God to make an entrance into this world, and with that entrance to give that revelation for which Judas Thaddeus pleads in our text?

CHAPTER 10

Shattered Values: Overcoming Dangerous Judgments

One of the Pharisees asked him to eat with him, and he went into the Pharisee's house, and took his place at table. And behold, a woman of the city, who was a sinner, when she learned that he was sitting at table in the Pharisee's house, brought an alabaster flask of ointment, and standing behind him at his feet, weeping, she began to wet his feet with her tears, and wiped them with the hair of her head, and kissed his feet, and anointed them with the ointment. Now when the Pharisee who had invited him saw it, he said to himself, "If this man were a prophet, he would have known who and what sort of woman this is who is touching him, for she is a sinner." And Jesus answering said to him, "Simon, I have something to say to you." And he answered, "What is it, Teacher?" "A certain creditor had two debtors; one owed five hundred denarii, and the other fifty. When they could not pay, he forgave them both. Now which of them will love him more?" Simon answered, "The one, I suppose, to whom he forgave more." And he said to him, "You have judged rightly." Then turning toward the woman he said to Simon, "Do you see this woman? I entered your house, you gave me no water for my feet, but she has wet my feet with her tears and wiped them with her hair. You gave me no kiss, but from the time I came in she has not ceased to kiss my feet. You did not anoint my head with oil, but she has anointed my feet with ointment. Therefore I tell you, her sins, which are many, are forgiven, for she loved much; but he who is forgiven little, loves little." And he said to her, "Your sins are forgiven." Then those who were at table with him began to say among themselves, "Who is this, who even forgives sins?" And he said to the woman, "Your faith has saved you; go in peace."

Luke 7:36–50

I never cease to be amazed by the colorful characters whom we meet in the Bible. They are not all alike and we are not dealing with painted saints. We do not encounter among them the same kind of reverent monotony we find in Eastern icons. They are thrown together in sharply contrasting mixes in this story of the Pharisee and the sinful woman. The same is true elsewhere. Among the poor, the lame, and the blind we find the rich young man who represented the cultural classes. There is Peter the activist and John the man of quiet thoughtfulness; the Pharisee and the publican. Even between Jesus and the two who shared with him the hill of Golgotha there are worlds of difference.

How is it that we find such? Or are they simply a depiction of life with all its contrasts?

It is not quite so simple. To be sure, even here there can be polar contrasts between rich and poor, gifted and foolish, educated and uneducated. Yet they are relativized, one can almost say remodeled: the rich man suddenly appears as poor—one has only to think of the story of Dives and Lazarus (Luke 16) in which the rich man perishes in his separation from God. On the other hand the mouths of the poor can be filled. The gifted and educated, the man of worldly wisdom can stand behind the children of God who are close to the heart of God.

Our text deals with a much deeper and more radical polarity. Here it is a matter of basic contrast of good and evil, and it is exciting to see how this contrast infiltrates, changes, and comes out in an entirely different light. The host in our text is a man of some reputation, a professional religionist who deals with the Word of God and who lives under the discipline of the commandments. He is what we call a good man. In contrast to him is someone from the world of shadows—known everywhere and of bad reputation. We know what she does for a living and with whom she consorts.

People call her "bad" or "a wicked woman." But in Jesus' eyes a reevaluation of current moral values appears to take place. On the gospel's scale of values do not those who sin with the senses come off better than those greedy practitioners of piety who pay their tithe as a gift to God? Who is really on the side of good and who of evil? Is it what we take to be an exchange, a contradiction, only a matter of a Christian's special gift that only belongs to those paradoxical peculiarities of the gospel and therefore hardly needs to concern anyone who is not familiar with such things? I incline to the idea that this is what is often the case when we consider and ponder the message of Jesus: the gospel also brings certain experiences to light, makes them known, and confirms experiences we have or can have in real life.

Here is a man who has wonderful health. The Mayo Clinic would look in vain for any evidence of illness. And yet this same man can be in very poor shape, depressed, burned out, empty, lonely. Perhaps the lack of health problems is what caused him to go to the clinic. Because everything went so well with that, he never had the opportunity to learn how to sympathize with others.

This calls to mind a very personal experience. When I was a student I had what in those days was regarded as a rather hopeless illness, which was not betrayed by my appearance. Because of this particular illness I was not able to submit a particular piece of academic work on time. When I tried to give an excuse for this to my professor he said: "Don't give sickness as an excuse and don't look for sympathy. Do you think fantastically healthy people are the only ones from whom we can expect anything? We ailing people [he himself was a sick man] have to give our all. We are the ones from whom God demands some accomplishment." At first I was furious with these remarks, but the memory of them has helped me many times. What I at first had perceived as an unjustified attack, the professor had meant as that exchange of values such as occurs in the message of Jesus. That is what we mean when we speak of the poor rich, the rich poor, and the healthy afflicted.

Nonetheless we must raise the question, Does the gospel really just tear down the distinction between good and evil—that is to say, does the gospel rescind all those norms which used to be important?

Jesus can still say to someone who has experienced his forgiveness: "Go and sin no more" (John 5:14; 8:11).

Here the sin is not called by name. The designation "evil" is not simply eradicated. And even in our text Jesus, by telling the parable, gives us to understand that this woman is in need of forgiveness and bears the burden of evil that has to be removed from her. This is not a matter of retouching the burden. And in spite of everything, at the end this woman appears as the one who is healthy (or the one who has become healthy); the Pharisee-host is the one who is really sick and who lacks what is necessary. We must try to understand these two figures more deeply. What was the Pharisee's sickness?

There is no doubt that he was a serious man, morally beyond reproach, spotless. What was so bad about him, what made him a disappointment to God? What is wrong with him lies so deeply in his humanity that it escapes the eye. The Pharisee is the kind of person who is pious and religious and who lives by certain moral standards and is surrounded by values which, in the last analysis, go back to the commandments of God but which are legally independent and which to an extent have degenerated. The commandments became empty abstract norms and hardly betray any hint of their original author, God. On the contrary, the idea of God is manipulated and modeled until it fits into the system of norms.

So one has—to cite an example—the idea of righteousness. If it is demanded of people that they live according to this idea, one would sooner expect that the source of all good and righteousness, that God himself, credibly incorporates this idea. How, then, should we conceive of him? Naturally we should conceive of God as the righteous God who corresponds to what we conceive of as righteousness—he must punish the bad and reward the good, as a just judge would do. But he does not do this. Often it goes very well with those who exploit and do injury to those whose faces are pressed into the mud (cf. Psalm 73). Job's entire complaint was that he had fashioned his God along these ideas of righteousness. Then, when a terrible series of catastrophes befalls Job, when God seems to punish him rather than to reward him for doing good, then

Job's concept of God has to fall apart and become the face of an unrighteous God which could drive one mad.

But often there are no such catastrophes which spoil this picture of a just God (i.e., a God whom one has fashioned according to one's own concept of righteousness). One can live quite comfortably and easily with this concept without noticing that one has a tailor-made God and is playing with an illusion. Perhaps the Pharisee-host of our text is such a man who lives in such a naive circumstance. We can guess how he conceived of God: God is at one with his party guests, with decent people, the pious, morally spotless people with the immaculate past. We want nothing to do with riffraff, murderers, thieves, perverts, and other scum. Even his people, for example, his church, seek to keep their distance from them. It can not be otherwise with a God who is formed according to the model concept of human righteousness.

Now questionable theological concepts are never entirely false. Elements of truth are to be found even in them. So it is here. From the correct assumption that God does not want sin we draw another conclusion, one that must derive from such a concept of God. That conclusion or consequence is this: If God does not want sin, neither does he want a sinner. He wants nothing to do with either. And because I want to be on God's side there has to be a wall of separation between me and the scum.

This is what must come of every self-secure, loveless attitude of the Pharisee who says to God: "God, I thank thee that I am not like other men, extortioners, unjust, adulterers, or even like this tax collector" (Luke 18:11). We know which of the two went down justified and which one heard God's rejection. The human, all-too-human picture of a righteous God permitted the Pharisee to forget that in the eyes of God the border between a righteous and an unrighteous man lies somewhere else entirely. The Pharisee's attempt to imprison God in the scheme of his ideas hid from him God's true nature—that he is a compassionate God who seeks man, with whom one sinner counts more than ninety-nine righteous who think they have no need of his healing attention. And by suggesting such a twisted idea of God they block the way to their neighbor. They cannot love their neighbor, they can only despise him. They concentrate on the speck in his eye and forget about the log in their own (Matt. 7:3). We come upon this tendency to judge, this self-righteousness of the faithful everywhere we go. Perhaps we are among them. This is not a matter of history of some time or other. We have people like this at all times and of course we have all manner of human ideas about God, into which we cram our ideas about God.

For all people whose presuppositions are fixed and rigid a figure such as Jesus is always a mystery. That is why the Pharisee thought: "If this man were a prophet, then. . . ." For him and his kind Jesus could not possibly be a prophet because he did not hold their view of the world and God and because he did not keep his distance from moral corruption, as in the case of the poor wretch of a woman who seems to be flattering him with her attention. No, Jesus cannot be a prophet because even the idea of a prophet is determined by given values. One can be a prophet only if he confirms that which is a binding norm in me. The human being is always given its impetus by the compulsion for self-assertion. I even control the criteria for what makes a prophet. How could it be otherwise when God himself is subject to my standards. So then it is impossible for anyone to be a prophet if he questions all my judgments. Our judgments are the most secure things—we know they are bomb-proof.

Anyone who is so caught up in his own "system," his own judgments and ideologies can no longer be astonished or surprised. For such a person there are no new perspectives that open up to him. He is, as I said, concerned only with justifying himself. People with such dogmatic fixations cannot live otherwise. That is what our ideologies hold before us every day. They do not permit their convictions to be shaken. Whatever is entirely new and cannot be accommodated by existing judgments is devalued. "This fellow cannot be a prophet . . . .

Jesus' love for sinners, his passion for their redemption—all that is entirely new: it just did not fit the Pharisees' way of thinking and therefore will be banned henceforth from consideration. To admit such a thought hithertofore would mean that one would have to revise the whole body of thought up to this point and turn everything upside down. Such a thing could make us dizzy and throw us into a vacuum.

What is attributed to us here, the host may think, does not allow itself to be brought into line with everything we hold sacred. That is not just a patch on the old clothing of our convictions (we would like that because we are willing to make corrections) that means that we must rather undress completely—and stand in the cold in order to be dressed anew. But how? Even the ones who are faithful to their convictions, the people with strong foundations, must regard Jesus as a threat, an assassin of all that is holy.

No, this fellow cannot be a prophet; he is not permitted to be a prophet. These people find it more difficult to get along with him than the uncertain, tortured souls or even the children who are not yet committed to anything. That is why those who are most secure can be among the poor and neediest.

These secure people have their dignity in spite of what they lack. It was not an easy matter for these Pharisees to become so doctrinaire; they came to their ideas at a great cost and they had sacrificed a great deal so that their life would conform to their doctrine. Although Jesus speaks very strictly, there is no doubt but that he loves them. Whoever cares about the poor also has compassion on those whose poverty is hidden under the cover of their wisdom, their loyalty of conviction, and by their confidence.

Nonetheless we must sense something deeper in the blemished development which emerges out of the Pharisee's false idea of God. The Pharisee is a representative figure and is not bound to the time period of the New Testament; rather he is a remaining present. To be fixed in his judgments—in this case his moral judgments—is the Pharisee's illness.

This illness spreads much like cancer. It attacks our self-judgment as well as our ability to judge other people and undermines both. Now the disease strikes erroneous judgments: a woman who becomes a prostitute—it is possible because she was seduced or because she or her family would starve otherwise—to Jesus she appears to be of better reputation than the nice gentlemen at his table who (naturally very discreetly) are not too scrupulous about their marital fidelity, or than those women who destroy unborn life but enjoy undisputed social status. In case the host has heard Jesus' parable of the Good Samaritan (Luke 10:30–37), then it was clear what kind of grades he would have to give. A collegial solidarity made the conduct of the priest and Levite seem understandable when they left the robbers' victim lying in the road. Perhaps they had to give a lecture in Jericho that evening—a lecture about love for our fellow man—and they were too pressed for time to dawdle with the beaten man. The only scoundrels in the story, of course, were the robbers who had assaulted and beaten their victim to a bloody pulp.

Does not the moral ruler (12-inch ruler), with which the host measures the greater and lesser departures from the norm, lead to completely other grades than those which God, the real God, hands out? Could it not be that in his eyes the priest and Levite would be judged for withholding their duty to their neighbor and be put to shame by a heathen Samaritan. And is it not also possible that God could have pity on the thugs because he saw what led them to do this deed: desperate poverty or because they were reared in an asocial environment?

There is no end to the wrong judgments one can make because of the Pharisee's understanding about God: even a murderer who kills a bloodsucker would appear to him to be more worthy of contempt than a common scold, a gossip who is forever spreading tales of rumor and gossip. All judgment which the Pharisee makes causes his whole orientation to become so gruesomely prominent and has nothing—absolutely nothing—to do with what God's eyes see when they look into the background. He wants to serve God and thinks he is speaking in God's name, but he grows farther and farther from God.

The figure of the sinful woman on the contrary is not established by fixed ideas. She has nothing in her hands: neither principles nor firmness. In her poverty and need for comfort she has only empty hands and confidence in the one who does not despise her but will raise her up. She can be concerned with something that is new. She can experience the miracle of forgiveness. She never would have been included in this miracle if she had not taken seriously the damning mortgage and debt of sin upon her life and regarded herself as the sinless victim of a social fate. Even that would have been prejudice which would have hindered her openness to Jesus and put her in a position like the one we noted with the Pharisee-host. After all, anyone who regards himself as the

victim of society's ills cannot want any forgiveness. How can something that was not a sin be forgiven when it indicated only a social
infection which cried out only for the overcoming of the infection.
One may not have a beam or a log in his eye but the body of society
is full of splinters.

No. Precisely because the woman does not relativize the contrast
between good and evil to her advantage but rather lets the contrast
stand, her release from the bondage of her chains is overwhelming—even ecstatic. She may acknowledge the Pharisee's scaled values; indeed, his values may even be hers, but unlike the Pharisee
she is not self-confident. On the contrary, she is rather insecure
and full of doubt. This is why she can be open for the miracle of
someone smashing the judgment of these stone tablets in order to
remove the burden of the former life and to give a new beginning
in order to save a life. She is forgiven not because she loves. Indeed,
it is the other way around. She loves him who freed her because
she was given so much forgiveness.

What does forgiveness consist of? Basically it consists of Jesus'
maintaining fellowship with those whose sin and guilt pain him.
The condition for this possibility of forgiveness is that Jesus dis-
tinguishes between sinners and sin. If he remains aloof from the
sin—and he does that—he does not stand aloof from the sinner.
When the psalmist in the midst of his struggles and temptation says
"Nevertheless I am continually with thee" (Ps. 73:23), then Jesus
says—between the lines—to the guilt-ridden man: "Continually—
even though you come from afar and the ravages of blasphemy
can be seen on your face—I am continually with you and declare
you free." The sinner is not an object of contempt to him but of
compassion: he was moved with compassion for the people because
they became faint and were scattered abroad as sheep without a
shepherd (Matt. 9:36). Forgiveness comes about like the continuing
reaction among guilt, reaction to punishment, and very deep involvement. The sinner no longer identifies with his past but sees
only what God intends for him.

Who then needs to be forgiven in our text? Not just the woman
who receives it with indescribable liberation. Forgiveness is intended for the Pharisee. Without a doubt Jesus wants to win him
and win fellowship with him and free him from the invisible chains

that threaten to impede Jesus' offer. Why else would Jesus have gone to the Pharisee's house? Was not Jesus' acceptance of the invitation into the Pharisee's house itself his offer? Was not his acceptance the assurance "I am ready for you"? And is not Jesus' gentle criticism of Simon's failure to provide an adequate reception in his home an expression of grief that Simon persevered in his restraint, at the same time an attempt to lure him out, and by the example of the woman to show him his great need for forgiveness? And the Pharisee himself? He does not seem to be as sure of himself as it would seem. Would he have invited Jesus into his home if there were no trace of expectation in him? Somehow he must have been a questioning person who found something lacking in his spiritual home. And this questioning was the first indication that Jesus had touched him. When the whole business of the woman took place and he saw his most fundamental principles placed under a question mark, it became clear to him what a turnaround of values was demanded of him; he is shocked and sobered and puts on the brakes which stop him in his tracks: "If this fellow Jesus were a prophet. . . ." But he is not a prophet and cannot be a prophet. I know that God is different and that his prophet would be completely different. So I do not have to become upset.

The worst part of this self-righteousness into which the Pharisee flees anew and which makes him immune to Jesus is probably not even the dreadful, inflated opinion of himself which belongs to self-righteousness, that is, the lack of humility, perhaps not even self-confidence. The worst is that the self-righteous person is damned to a life of lovelessness. The only question that interests him as far as other people are concerned is: Do you conform to the norms which are valid to me? (If so, you are one of mine.) Or do you live by other norms and standards? (In which case I do not accept you.)

So, then, the spiritual disease of the religious pious is self-righteousness. Who would not have been afflicted with it who has come in contact with it? This ailment weakens by infecting others with its belief that it has something to appeal to them. This ailment impedes the missionary power that wins or wants to win souls. The self-righteous person is the type satirized by Nietzsche, who does not seem saved enough when he represents the proclaimed savior credibly. The self-righteous remain apart by themselves because it is only in their own circle that they find the security they seek and need and do not have to submit to any kind of disturbance or question. They become murky streams that are not fed by fresh streams and have no overflow. The self-righteous person who cannot love and also be open is not able to meet that aggravating distinction which contains the key to the saving gospel and Jesus' saving work—I mean the distinction between the sin and the sinner.

In his novel *Crime and Punishment* Dostoevski offers a parallel to the account in our text. Here he tells about Sonia, a girl who became a prostitute for the sake of her desperately impoverished parents and who reads to the despairing murderer, Raskolnikov, the story of the raising of Lazarus, which saves him. We can love Sonia the prostitute. From her we can learn the distinction between prostitution and one who is prostituted. She, too, is a human being; her hands are empty, but she is open to the grace which she so gratefully praises and which restores her health. It is because of her great gratitude that the woman offers her the gift of expensive nard. In the case of the resurrection of a life which had died—and this is what it is all about here—all calculation and figuring about what else could have been done with the money spent for the nard has no place (Jesus rebukes his disciples when they begin to speculate along this line [Matt. 26:9]). The great churches and cathedrals are signs in stone of such gratitude. Love of God and love of neighbor are not to be separated from each other. Still, there must be moments when we are overwhelmed by gifts of grace and we are compelled to forget our budgets; we have to splurge.

CHAPTER 11

Seed and Harvest

The point is this: he who sows sparingly will also reap sparingly, and he who sows bountifully will also reap bountifully. Each one must do as he has made up his mind, not reluctantly or under compulsion, for God loves a cheerful giver. And God is able to provide you with every blessing in abundance, so that you may always have enough of everything and may provide in abundance for every good work. As it is written,

> "He scatters abroad, he gives to the poor;
> his righteousness endures for ever."

He who supplies seed to the sower and bread for food will supply and multiply your resources and increase the harvest of your righteousness. You will be enriched in every way for great generosity, which through us will produce thanksgiving to God.

2 Cor. 9:6–11

Seed and harvest are powerful, parabolic pictures of great strength. In these pictures the Word becomes the seed that is sown in good soil but which can also fall on hard and rocky ground where it can come to naught. The teacher of youth spreads his seed in hope and in many cases he never sees the fruit that comes from the seed. There is always a distinction between success and fruit. Full barns—great success in the fields—can be success but they can also be fruitless and without blessing, as in the case of the wealthy farmer (Luke 12:16–21). The day of harvest which we celebrate every day directs our thought to the original happening of seed and harvest which turn up even anew under these figures.

This cannot happen, of course, unless we think about our present-day situation and become clear about how far our consciousness has strayed from that original happening.

Harvest and thanks for the harvest have become very strange to us. The law of life in urban areas, urbanization, and technical civilization have alienated us from the natural processes of life. Who stops to think about the fields and what grows and rots on them between the mountains of concrete and the clouds of automobile dust in the big cities?

But the belief in the makability of all things, in the *homo faber* in the machine age, makes it difficult for us to think about harvest— about thanksgiving and plowing fields and scattering good seed on the land. Certainly growth and prosperity is expected less from the hand of heaven than from artificial fertilizer and price supports and farm banks.

Finally, a very realistic economic consideration confronts us with the difficulty of thinking about such things as thanksgiving and harvest.

Indeed, we are even confronted by the shocking question of whether good harvests are a blessing. Do we not speak on the one hand of surpluses of meat and butter, and on the other hand of the contrast in areas of great hunger? Every day television shows us hungry children with bodies thin as rails and with bloated bellies.

Does nothing that we have learned about the blessing of the harvest as gifts of God have any meaning today?

If blessing turns into curse, does it not seem to be unavoidable that we separate ourselves from the idea, which people used to hold in more naive and less complex times, that there is one who blesses? Does one not feel compelled to say there is no such thing as blessing. There is only calculation and balances of supply and demand. There is only the law of market involvements and its opposite.

Could it not also be maintained that by no means was it the one who blessed but rather we men who have been blind and been blinded? Every alert observance of history compels us to ask this question.

I must mention yet one more scruple over against an all-too-naive idea of harvest thanksgiving: do not the biblical concepts of seed and harvest, of sheep and wolves, day and night, the lilies of the field and the birds of the heavens originate from a more childish time when we were closer to nature, whereas in our day we overcome the difference between day and night, heat and cold, by electricity?

We must speak here of our attitude toward nature. Here I want to say this. Whoever reads the great creation and nature psalms (e.g., Psalm 104) immediately gets the impression that there is everything but a romantic relationship to nature. The ocean, for example, is a symbol of terror and of the upheaval of the elements, that storm, fire and flame, and earthquake is what is meant. Above all the biblical witness of nature is characterized by this: in them neither nature nor creation as a whole but rather the Creator himself is addressed: "From the womb of the morning like dew your youth will come to you" (Ps. 110:3); "thou takest away their breath, they die and return to their dust" (Ps. 104:29); "for he makes his sun rise on the evil and on the good, and sends rain on the just and on the unjust" (Matt. 5:45).

Whoever busies himself with nature alone finds himself confronted with nothing but contradictions at the outset. That is the miracle of conception and birth; but it is a thousandfold dying. Here we have a bright spring valley; but at the same time in the midst there is also a chasing and a being chased, the joy of the booty and the death cry of the booty.

We experience what blessing is not simply from sheer encounter with creation; one experiences blessing before the countenance of the very one who blesses, whose word speaks and enlightens the higher thoughts and the puzzles of contradictions. To be sure, we can see so much in God's footsteps in nature that touches us as miracle and moves us to reverence. But what we see does not tell us whose steps we see, nor who it is to whom those clues point.

In light of this *You* who speaks to us and blesses us behind all the processes of nature, we want to think about the question of whether and why the picture of seed and harvest continues to concern us.

To begin with our text shows that the thought of one who blesses awakens in us the sense of humility: it is God who comes to us in gifts of great generosity. He lets us have enough of everything and so puts us in the position to overflow in acts of goodness and giving (2 Cor. 9:8). In this there is a strong hint that we mortals simply cannot make many things. For example, we cannot make ourselves to be other than what we are. We cannot add to our stature (Matt. 6:27). Nor can we do anything we have not been given the power to do.

The same is true of humility: we must accept ourselves as we are. We cannot make ourselves over. At harvest time, and most especially on the day of Thanksgiving, we are especially reminded that we cannot control the weather, that moisture, rain, and sunshine are really in God's hands.

Of course, the idea occupies us—we dare not retreat too easily or quickly to the spiritual realm—whether someday we will not be able to influence the weather and win from God yet another privilege. In case it should come to that we will see what we also see in the field of medicine: what we mortals think to undertake on the basis of what we are able to do is not something we simply snatch from the roll of the dice and bring into some kind of systematic order, it can lead to strange contradictions. We can struggle against infant mortality which can promote the population explosion and produce a host of hunger catastrophes. That is just one of many possible examples that show us what can happen when mortals make themselves junior partners in God's firm and take over his books and accounts.

The person who uses God's gifts in his or her own name and who has lost the *You* is like the prodigal son of Jesus' parable. Everything he has is from the Father and he knows it. He consumes it blindly for himself without giving any thought to why or for what purpose the Father gave it to him. Is this not something comparable to our agricultural economy in which our technical and scientific gifts increase the production to a point of overproduction, a point where borrowed capital brings tremendous dividends without—to the Father's heartbreak—being shared by millions of his children in other parts of his world, children who will have to die of starvation? Woe to him who deals so selfishly and greedily with the Father's capital! The gift which does not remind us of the Giver and his intention but rather is used to the recipient's own purposes and ends rots in his hand, and instead of being a gift it becomes a curse.

Every year at the festival of Thanksgiving the lead articles in the press speak thanks to the farmers and occasionally to the biologist and the agricultural scientist. It would not be right to make little of their labor. Anyone who knows how hard they work and how meager their compensation is by comparison gladly joins in singing their praises. Our text points to an outlook that we all too easily forget, much to our own misfortune: that the farmer did not make the seed but that it is given to him and that all our other gifts and energy and ability and planning are not of man's making but have been given to us as a gift.

That is a very simple hint which we tend to overlook in an even simpler way. I remember that I once said to a student to whom I had given an excellent grade: "You are a gifted young fellow!" He blushed at that because he felt his intellectual faculties were being praised. I laughed and called attention to the fact that I had not said "You are a fantastic fellow" but that I had praised his gifts. To be gifted means that one has been showered with gifts one has not deserved to receive. So that student did not need to blush because actually I was not praising him with my words.

Who stops to think that with all our ingenuity brings to pass that the giver of all good gifts was at work?

Paul takes the step from the original seed—harvest—happening on the field to his parabolic use: he says that we are a seed which shall sprout up. One does not need to command this seed to rise up; it will do so of itself because that is its nature. Sprouting up is a spontaneous act. Precisely this spontaneity is given only to him who stands before the Giver of all good gifts as one who receives with gratitude. In this way such a person becomes what Paul calls a cheerful giver—someone who is driven to give because he himself has received so much—such a person rises up as seed.

One can easily imagine what a revolution that means in our life. For the giving of which Paul speaks here is usually characterized by the slogan "As you do to me, I do to you."

But here it is not what I offer for disposal that is a standard (i.e., gift and corresponding deed). Rather is it the gift of God which becomes the criterion.

Then I am no longer bounded to the law of calculation and mere exchange of interest. God measures his gifts not by the inch, especially not by what we give him. God is generous. He who entrusts himself to God's generosity and gratefully keeps that generosity in mind in turn becomes generous. Such a person thinks also that God not only gives gifts but that in Jesus Christ God gives himself. Whoever conforms to Jesus' impression is quickly able to give himself. He will not want to separate his bank account from his full personal participation. To branch off onto a political line of thought, he will not consider it enough for our country just to put credit and machinery at the disposal of developing nations (and then frequently experience the disappointment that the recipients either do little or the wrong thing) but will feel moved personally to help these areas to become ready for such gifts.

One does not need to command the seed to rise. The seed does it, as we have said, of its own accord. The seed can be choked by thorns and be strewn on rocky ground (Mark 4:7, 18). We know too well where these choking powers work today. We need think only of stress and pressure to know what that means and what keeps us from coming to our senses and being concerned about the one thing that is needful to go to work in our lives.

The fall festival of the harvest reminds us how necessary it is to give thought to what is central and to give thought and effort to be thankful to him from whom every blessing comes. He wishes nothing more sincerely than that we know him as the one who blesses, not as our personal capital. Only he who gives thanks does not perish with the gift for which he gives thanks.

Luther's Small Catechism says: It is our task to make ourselves alert. "God gives us our daily bread without our asking, even to the wicked. But on this prayer we ask that he let us recognize and receive his gift with thanksgiving." Every day calls us to meditate upon this. That belongs to the "race that is set before us" (Heb. 12:1). And this is a race, a struggle because it is an ongoing hand-to-hand combat that is expected of us and it besets us steadily with reality and intensity that gives little time for meditative quiet. This calls for discipline and a sense of service to God quite apart from professional service of God. We just have to set aside a fixed time of the day for thinking. What our earthly profession demands of us is also required by God.

Whoever conforms to this offer and prescription will soon see what a blessing and power issue from it. In those daily moments we are like a piece of land that is not constantly cultivated but whose fruitfulness is increased by its "Sabbath rest."

The prayer's petition, "Give us this day our daily bread," points also to how God gives us his gifts. Jesus challenges us to ask only for a day's ration of bread, not for so many pounds of bread and other quantities of food which we could use in the course of a lifetime. He does not tell us to ask for tomorrow and the day after. We could get the idea that this once-and-for-all prayer is an all-inclusive prayer and let it go at that. We could perceive our being satisfied to be a normal condition and simply forget him upon whom our life depends (John 6:26).

When Jesus challenges us to be content to ask only for rations for the day he draws a parallel between God's bread and God's Word. To be sure, the Word of God is a light to our path which is meant to enlighten the farthest distance of the future (Ps. 37:25). At the same time it is a light to our feet for only the next step, leading us in the darkness only step by step into the light.

The Word of God is not a floodlight! We hold God's hand and follow him step by step into the darkness. We do not see through the darkness, but God knows the way. And that is enough light for our next step.

We can be content to pray only for the very next because we are certain that this whole life with its peaks and valleys is in God's hands. The rainbow of reconciliation embraces from horizon to horizon. We can see God behind the darkest clouds (Gen. 9:14) and understand him as the promise that so long as the earth stands, there shall be seed and harvest, heat and cold, summer and winter, day and night (Gen. 8:22). As if in a vision the cosmonauts were privileged to see our earth in a unique way and they called the earth the "greening star" which shines out of the midst of the universe's darkness.

It would be irresponsible if we did not add here a word of self-criticism: Have we not turned faith into cheap optimism? Did not God also permit an Auschwitz to be constructed on this green star?

Can we still praise him "who so wondrously reigneth"? Are there not moments when such praise must pale before the deaths of innocent children from napalm and automobile wheels? How can he who brings the harvest from seed also send hail with spring?

God's rainbow stands over all things. We cannot see his hand at work or explain how he does what he does. But we do see those people of God who catch this will to be. They dared to trust that the God who had drawn near to them in Jesus Christ would show his power even in the hour of darkness. They saw no meaning but they trusted in him that there is meaning. Thus, their cry of lamentation became a hymn of praise. Thanks and praise find their way to the heart of God not only via receiving gifts that bring good fortune but in hours of trial and despair and depression.

Perhaps we can see from this that thanks for a harvest is not only a matter of nature and seed and harvest, a natural process. Wherever we look—in the clouds, mountains, sea, fields, woods—we confront the question, "Who are you? What do you trust and believe in?" But there is another question, too: "I did that for you; what do you do for me?" We hear this question only if we do not stick to mere appearences but hear the Word of him who "gives wind and wave their course and way" and who says to us in his Word that he wants to be my own and that I should belong to him.

CHAPTER 12

The End of the World

And there will be signs in sun and moon and stars, and upon the earth distress of nations in perplexity at the roaring of the sea and the waves, men fainting with fear and with foreboding of what is coming on the world; for the powers of the heavens will be shaken. And then they will see the Son of man coming in a cloud with power and great glory. Now when these things begin to take place, look up and raise your heads, because your redemption is drawing near." And he told them a parable: "Look at the fig tree, and all the trees; as soon as they come out in leaf, you see for yourselves and know that summer is already near. So also, when you see these things taking place, you know that the kingdom of God is near. Truly, I say to you, this generation will not pass away till all this has taken place. Heaven and earth will pass away, but my words will not pass away. But take heed to yourselves lest your hearts be weighed down with dissipation and drunkenness and cares of this life, and that day come upon you suddenly like a snare; for it will come upon all who dwell upon the face of the whole earth. But watch at all times, praying that you may have strength to escape all these things that will take place, and to stand before the Son of man.

Luke 21:25–36

Just how seriously do we take the prayer, "thy kingdom come"? Do we not spout this petition without any serious thought? This powerful text tells us what the Lord's Prayer means when it speaks of the coming kingdom of God. We need this commentary as a steady companion lest the Lord's Prayer become a meaningless collection of pious phrases.

The church year portrays in microcosm the entire panorama of salvation history. That is why its concluding phase is governed by gospel texts that speak of the end of the world. Our text is to be seen in the light of this message. But here the tone and climate are substantially altered. Over the darkness over the huge grave of the world there bursts an advent light. Before everything stood under the sign of a judgment harvest, of the call to conversion, and of the ax laid to the roots of the tree. But now there is a tone of cheerful expectation of the end: Lift up your heads, the Lord is at hand. The old world is groaning in its agony. But the door of the great death chamber is opened and a worthy figure (John Paul I) has stepped in. The joy that this is the way it is and is going to be is the tenor of our story. Our ear must be trained to hear this tone.

Probably our hearing is not attuned to this frequency. I am not thinking about the so-called people of the world for whom this age is everything who never think anything of the beyond.

I am thinking in particular about Christians and not simply about those who are Christians in name only—people with baptismal certificates, the corpses of membership lists, but also active Christians, people who want to be earnest Christians.

For a long time—and not just under the influence of important theologians—we have been pondering our affirmation of our worldliness and discussed what it is that God expects of us. Jesus Christ was and is the assertion who wants to encounter us in the middle of our life and not just on the boundaries of life or in border situations of particular needs and despairs. He wants to be a Good Samaritan and the one driven by love to change the world here and now in the midst of our normal everyday life. To this, our earthly here and now, is what we are turned to and not some coming day, that day which is the end of all things, so as not to lose ourselves in some apocalyptic otherworldliness. The lilies of the field become the symbols which make our present holy. We should still want (as Luther is reputed to have said) to plant our apple tree today even if we knew tomorrow were the end of the world.

Our glance toward the "other side" is not a stubborn one, that of what awaits us on the other side of death's boundary, diverting us from what God gives us today. That is why early Christians used to say "There is also a life before death." That is something very much worth thinking about. What can all that our text says about the end of the world mean, what kind of power resides in it? We find that more readily if we first become clear about what the passage cannot mean.

Jesus' word about the end of the world is considerably different than what Oswald Spengler had to say about the "Decline of the West." Here we see ourselves caught up in the same cycle of becoming and passing away as we first find it in the change of seasons. Even cultures come and go. They have their spring and the heat of summer, the last glow of fall, and finally their growing numb and their end. So it is not a matter of a sudden collapse. For there will always be new generations which will walk over the graves of the old.

What Jesus means here is the complete end, the unedited end. The song of the birds will be silenced. Mozart's *Little Night Music* will no longer sound forth—nor will any chorales. The lilies of the field are burned. This age goes forth to its end in catastrophes, the most decisive of which is this.

Here there is not the faintest hint of a pessimism that would declare our world will collapse into nothing and simply dissolve into atomic fires. No! The world will break up, paradoxically, from an unheard-of fulfillment. Here it is not simply a matter of going to the end but of the future as one that is coming to us: it is a matter of the exalted Lord coming to us for a second time. The human Tower of Babel which boasts of man's own power does not simply blow apart so that we can not be seen because of dust and smoke, but above the ruins the Lord appears. That is why at this end we hear not the nihilist's cry of "Let us eat and drink, for tomorrow we die" (1 Cor. 15:32) but the shout of joy: "Lift up your heads; your redemption draws nigh."

But even here we have not reached the actual depth of the text. We have just touched upon the mood that is awakened in us by the text. We have spoken of the—shall we say—courage of Daniel in the lions' den. But how did he get this courage? We have noticed the composure and coolness of those who become aware of the signs of catastrophe in the moon and the stars. But what gives them this composure? What should these signs do for us? We saw our-selves directed to the sobriety of waiting in the midst of a drunken world that seeks its comfort in forgetting and in illusions. But how do the saints come to this sobriety of hope? If we only find some-thing like a euphoric mood, a climate of positiveness in our text we miss its points. And whenever possible we let Christ's coming only be a mythical projection of our mood of hope, a visionary overview of that principle of hope which constitutes an element that cannot be lost of our being a human being.

The key for our being able to understand that in the midst of the world's passing and collapse we can pass over into the advent of forejoy and hold our heads high is the certainty that the kingdom of God must surely come when all the kingdoms of this earth cease and God's hour strikes when all earthly clocks stop running.

This is so elementary that it could be stated thusly: this gener-ation, of which I announce the end of the old and the beginning of the new, will not pass away until everything has come to pass. There is a special theological phrase that has been coined for this; it is called the "prophetic abbreviation of the time perspective" and means that there is something akin to a prophetic telescope that shows what is coming to be very near. The intensity of waiting for fulfillment bridges the temporal gaps that still separate us from the fulfillment.

Nor does this text want to infect us with a mood or lull us into one, but rather it cites hard and real reasons that bring about a mood of comfort and good spirit. The main reason is, the Lord is nigh: he will come down from heaven and land among those who stand about him and hear this announcement.

It is very difficult and harsh when one says it this way. Could that which for Jesus' listeners was a great inspiration be a great discouragement for us? Could we then—if we are honest—ex post facto realize that the Lord will come again and will appear with his saints and all believers on this great day (2 Thess. 1:10)?

The negative side of the promise—the word of the collapses to come—enlightens us even sooner: we sense the world's coming apart at the seams; we see the instability of the constellations of powers; we know the destructive potency locked up in atomic weaponry, the collapse of the norms of our world, the polarization of political powers, the escalation of brutality, and many other things. The fruitless fig tree does not simply bear, it bears poisoned fruit. We see it all; on that we can agree.

But if it is an announcement of the Lord who is coming again, does the announcement really have the quality of a harbinger? Have there not always been similar earthquakes, and have not men always awaited Christ's second coming because they believed they could see the harbingers of his coming? And yet he did not come. The earthquakes calmed and the rhythm of the seasons continued as before as though nothing had happened.

Again, can we cause such a hope to come to pass in us? If we cannot, then we should be honest and dissociate ourselves from the mood of the text and become outright nihilists.

To this core question I would like to point to two thoughts without developing them. My only concern is to incite impulses for one's consideration.

The first thought: It is very significant that first in the prophets, then in the gospels, and finally in Christianity in general, we come to the conclusion that we find the final judgment in certain terrors and afflictions of that particular time. Yes, the end of the world casts its shadow before. The large hand of the world clock has really stood at twelve o'clock and will continue to move as though nothing had happened. At the same time the most decisive thing has happened already (Matt. 24:36; 1 Thess. 5:1ff.).

As little as we recognize the arrival of the midnight hour of the end of the world and of the second coming (therefore we must grow to the hour (Matt. 24:42; 25:1ff.; Luke 12:40) the more the signs of the times and the previews of the big hand are discerned in the terrible events of history. It was in this sense that Jesus pointed to the event of the flood in Matt. 24:37–41.

As a matter of fact one of these calamities is the one before the last. Thus the final judgment of Sodom and Gomorrah was pre-

ceded by the invasion of the kings from the east (Gen. 14:1ff.;
19:24f.). The final destruction of Jerusalem was preceded by the
invasion from the north prophesied by Joel. And Antiochus, who
commanded this invasion, closed the temple for the time being,
both of which were portentous events. Behind this next-to-last catastrophe there always rises the last (even though it may only rank
as next-to-last). One needs only to think of the once-flourishing
showplaces of the early churches in Asia Minor and Africa that
have lost the light of the gospel and were passed over by what
Luther called the "flood rains" of the gospel.

The second thought: It always seems that when people think of
the end of the world and the second coming of the Lord "in this
generation" there is something that strikes the detached observer
as incomprehensible. People have tried all kinds of biblical number-
combinations to come upon the date for the second coming—even
to the hour of the day. (In this respect the great biblical theologian,
Albrecht Bengel, went awry when he calculated the date of the
millennium as 18 June 1836). At the appointed hour people would
go out to meet the Lord with prayers and hymns. Sometimes they
expected him to come at dawn on a mountain top. But he did not
come, and that day came and went as did all the others. Then
people turned around and went about their business and continued
to wait. To the eye of a worldling that must have been incomprehensible because it made fools of the believers. Was this not a
repudiation of one's faith? Why did that seem to go ignored by
these people while they continued to hope as if the disappointment
had not happened? That is a puzzle!

Let me point to a completely worldly example which can solve
this puzzle.

During the war I belonged to an anti-Nazi group whose leader
was Carl Goerdeler who was executed after the assassination plot
of 20 June 1944. We came together to work on an essay about how
to bring about the reorganization of Germany after the collapse
we all expected. Goerdeler, who had access to sources of information including how things stood with the war, was quite certain
that the collapse would come within the next three months. But
the end did not come. Three months later we sat with Goerdeler
again, and again he made the same prophecy. I was deeply touched

and I recall that no one accused him of misleading us about our time schedule or said that we would not be sitting there if he had been right the last time. I found myself entranced as I listened to his new proposals—and I believed them. It is not as though everything he had prophesied had been wrong. He had understood the developments of the war that were yet to come and events proved him right. Only his dates were incorrect. The end was always a bit farther off.

Only later did it become clear to me how all this was to be explained, especially the perplexing connection between a factually correct prognosis and at the same time an erroneous fixing of dates. Moreover neither Goerdeler nor the rest of us who listened to him felt any sense of ridicule. What happened was what I called the prophetic shortening of the time perspective. At that time the Battle of Stalingrad was just behind us. Stalingrad was the turning point of the war and the beginning of the end for Germany. After that everything was a lost cause. Goerdeler saw all this clearly. Precisely because his prognosis of the historical situation was correct this abbreviation of perspectives developed. It was an illustration of his correctness.

I asked if Jesus' statement that this generation would not pass until the end of the world came to pass and its subsequent expectations of the imminence of the second coming did not point to similar circumstances. In Jesus' appearance the "kingdom of God is in the midst of you" (Luke 17:21). From now on nothing—neither life nor angels nor powers nor principalities nor things present nor things to come—can separate us from the love of God which has appeared in Jesus (Rom. 8:38–39).

The resurrection of Christ is the real day of victory, the Stalingrad of history. Whatever happens after that—measured against the event—has no specific weight of its own. Nothing is able to come between us and God. Now, come what may, the earth is the Lord's (Ps. 24:1; 1 Cor. 10:26). The Word of the Lord has mastered it and remain its master even if heaven and earth pass away (Matt. 24:35). John, the Seer of Patmos, sees the new heaven and the new earth near at hand (Rev. 21:1).

When history is seen this way, in the light of the great day of victory, the far-off day of judgment becomes very close at hand.

The alarm of the end compels us to watchfulness, to the casting off heavy burdens that weigh down, to have as though we had not for the time is short (1 Corinthians 7:29–31).

Even wrong time-settings for the end of the world such as we have seen throughout history are only the reverse side of the coin, a show of history that is close to the heart of the gospel. That alone might be the reason why those terminal chronologies are not a history of disgrace. It was the conviction that the decisive battle has already taken place and that the end is in sight that one can survive all the crises of expectation.

The early church struggled with such questions about the closeness or distance of the end. To all who saw the end near at hand when history rolled on undisturbed as though nothing had happened 2 Peter offers these words of comfort: "The Lord is not slow about his promise as some count slowness, but is forbearing toward you, not wishing that any should perish, but that all should reach repentance. But the day of the Lord will come like a thief, and then . . . the earth and the works that are upon it will be burned up. . . . But . . . we wait for new heavens and a new earth . . ." (2 Peter 3:9–10, 13). While we wonder about God and ask "What is taking you so long—are you coming Godot?" God is thinking about us and asks "When are you going to reach the point when I finally can come?"

PART THREE

GOD—OUR HELPER
AGAINST DOUBT, ANXIETY,
AND DEATH

CHAPTER 13

Love Is Stronger
than Death

When they had finished breakfast, Jesus said to Simon Peter, "Simon, son of John, do you love me more than these?" He said to him, "Yes, Lord; you know that I love you." He said to him, "Feed my lambs." A second time he said to him, "Simon, son of John, do you love me?" He said to him, "Yes, Lord; you know that I love you." He said to him, "Tend my sheep." He said to him the third time, "Simon, son of John, do you love me?" Peter was grieved because he said to him the third time, "Do you love me?" And he said to him, "Lord, you know everything; you know that I love you." Jesus said to him, "Feed my sheep. Truly, truly, I say to you, when you were young, you girded yourself and walked where you would; but when you are old, you will stretch out your hands, and another will gird you and carry you where you do not wish to go." (This he said to show by what death he was to glorify God.) And after this he said to him, "Follow me."

John 21:15–19

What is old has passed away; everything has become new, Paul says in 2 Cor. 5:17. That is quite a statement to make. Only if one takes it seriously and tries to plumb its depths does one come upon the Easter secrets. The Lord himself has become different. Humility, suffering, and death are behind him. He has risen to majesty and sits enthroned on high. We may well complain about the retreat of Christian life from the public scene into the ghetto. We may complain that the newspapers and media report on everything but

him. They report the terrorism in the Near East and Northern
Ireland, of political intrigue and athletic contests, or the beauty
tips or the bedroom exploits of the stars. Nothing is too trite, nothing too dreadful to offer to the public's attention. But Jesus is still
the most despised because he is the one most silenced by death.
Yet he sits in all his Easter glory and oversees his plans with all of
us. This plan takes all of life's trivia, dreadfulness, and banality
into consideration. Even those who are shocked or fascinated, together with those who report these things, are not aware of it. Not
only are all things different with the Lord, they are different with
those who are his. Their lives have a new beginning. We see that
in a figure like Peter. The old that has passed away and is no more
with him is that scene of the threefold denial of Christ in the high
priest's courtyard and his tempermental exuberances are his panic
and flight when the crucified One hung between heaven and earth.
But now his life has a new beginning; his old mortgages have been
paid off. He looks from what is passed and gone to what is ahead
and coming.

What is in store for him in this new world age that has come to
pass?

First it must be said that Peter remains the rock on which the
Lord will build his church. He is thrice confirmed in his pastoral
office. He is to carry a tremendous responsibility for the flock.

Peter stands for all who are responsible for overseeing a duty in
the church of Christ, not only for those who hold an administrative
office—for bishops, pastors, and lay leaders of all kinds—but also
for the lonely Christian who lives as the only one who knows what
is going on among ignorant and apathetic colleagues and who seeks
to be responsible to his Lord. As our story shows, this responsibility
is conferred by the Lord himself and stems from none other. Neg-
atively speaking that means this responsibility is not an authority
conferred upon the dues-paying members of the church or by some
official or other. If that were the case we would—in our culture—
have to choose them in a democratic fashion. In that case the spirit
of the times would probably compete with the Holy Spirit for command of the church: abolish doctrine and dogma with their my-
thologies and the whole Old Testament (the Nazis tried that). That
stuff is not in keeping with the times. Never mind that business of

a utopia on the other side of the grave, that beautifully ordered kingdom of God. Concentrate rather on the realistic solving of this world's problems! Vote for the separation of faith through an ethical world order. Stop wearing the countenance of martyrs and get to work changing the world. That is what the spirit of the times demands; that is what we want. That is what the democratically understood church would say. But we do not have our charge from those who say this! We must resist them. If it is from the Lord that our charge comes then we must preserve and protect what has been entrusted to us, above all a truth in light of which the idols and favorite dreams of men are exposed and the way to freedom from their dictates is shown.

Peter—and with him all who have been given some responsibility—comes through that, into a difficult situation. Naturally he does not want to be an opportunist and trim his sails according to the wind. That would lead only to a fourth denial. But he wanted to be up-to-date if we want to use him as the personification of a modern preacher or of the institutional church. He does not do this to make himself popular but rather so that modern man will understand him and above all not be won to the idea that faith makes progress and thinking incompatible and that one has to leave his intellect at the church door. Did not Paul want to be a Jew to the Jews and a Greek to the Greeks in order to win both and to reach both? Of course he did. But he steadfastly refused as the great theologian, Martin Kaehler, once tellingly put it: Paul wanted to be a miracle worker to the Jews and a cultural Christian to the Greeks.

The fetching maneuver should not go so far that, without regard to losses or watering down, preaching his gospel could suit everyone. If he could have given his contemporaries a simple self-approval he would have won quite a few and for the time being had a great success. For people really desire self-approval (approval of themselves)—even we ourselves. But there would be an end to that as soon as people realized that these pieces of wisdom were without Christian witness. There is a fine line between being contemporary and belonging to the times; between the majesty of the Lord and the realm into which the spirit of the times, the usurper of this world, seeks to entice us.

The decision before which the commission of Peter places us suggests another point which has already been mentioned once before. In our day the word "democratization" exercises a certain magical power. It seems to be an open sesame for a new and enlightened world. One wants to admit the presumed blessing of this magic word into the whole church of Jesus Christ. That is why the ideological advocates of that word reject every vis-à-vis of shepherd and flock. They take it for authoritarianism (another magic word!) which contradicts the maturity promised by the "universal priesthood." As we said that is how it seems. And yet there must be this vis-à-vis between shepherd and flock if one is to be clear about the fact that we have received our commission to proclaim and teach directly from the flock. (That is of course no defense for the absolutizing of hierarchical structures!) In the spell of that magic word of democratization many officeholders in the church no longer want to be shepherds but "top sheep," members of the flock with which they are in solidarity and with whom they do not come into conflict. The opportunist who tries to accommodate himself everywhere avoids a shepherd's responsibility. His sole concern is to accommodate himself. But in the eyes of those from whom he has received his appointment he is not the top sheep but a faithless shepherd. Peter's denial is repeated ever anew.

How does one bear the responsibility of a shepherd? To put it another way—from whence does a shepherd derive his authority? Is he possessed of a greater insight? Or does he possess a greater measure of truth and—among other things—a theological education?

Jesus treats the privilege of the office of a shepherd but not by the question, Are you more intelligent? Is your I.Q. higher than some other disciple's so that I can regard you as being more competent of being a shepherd? Are you more loving? None of this qualifies you to be a shepherd.

This question is so decisive for this office that Jesus puts the question to Peter and even puts up with Peter's sorrow which asserts itself in the repetition of his question. He is very depressed because the Lord does not accept his spontaneous confession "Yes, I love you" immediately because he apparently still doubts him. Peter could have argued his denial. Had he not (and even before his denial) vowed his faithfulness? And what happened then?

The human heart is fickle. Its love can be put to tests for which
it is not suited. Yet this time Peter is not mistaken. He relies on
Jesus' omniscience to which no corners of his heart are hidden.
And before this penetrating look of his Lord he pledges: there is
no corner of my life which is not permeated by his love.

What is this love like? I love my friends. I love certain books. I
even love my car. But this kind of love can hardly be meant here.
What kind of love then is meant? I can only love when I know that
I am loved and accepted, when love is unleashed in me. Whoever
has not experienced love or known what it is to be accepted—one
need only to think of the sad experiences with juvenile delin-
quency—has instead of the natural potential for love a drive of
aggressiveness. Our inner energies, even the energy of Love, are
ambivalent; they can at any time turn into the opposite. But Peter
is one who knows he is accepted. And in this experience which
sustains and shapes him, Jesus is his person of reference for he
accepts Peter in spite of his disloyalty and even in the midst of it.
That Jesus holds on to him in spite of his denial gives birth to a
deeper tie to the Lord than mere sympathy could have brought
about. What happened on the cross where Jesus died for the godless
and accepted them gives to this confrontation its deepest meaning.

In the same sense intended by Jesus is a completely human picture, for Jesus is also a human being just as we are (cf. Heb. 4:15).
This love is released in me when I follow the way of the Lord—
his sympathy in suffering, his compassion, his sacrifice, his unerring
loyalty. When the Roman Catholic initiates his stations of the cross
and immerses himself in blood and wounds, then that is an ex-
citement of love. Once at a Good Friday service I attended the
children brought flowers and laid them before the feet of the figure
of the crucified Lord. That was an expression of this love. This
love sought to identify with the man of pain and to thank him.

At this point I ask myself quite critically if I am not drifting off
into the psychic and saying something sentimental, if I am not
departing from the sober line of a spiritual meditation. Rudolph
Bultmann is just such a sensitive interpreter of Scripture who would
hold that up to me. That he is opposed to such psychic, sensitive
understanding of love expresses itself in his critique of our text.
Here he turns against the business of feeling that appears to be

inherent in the comparative phrase "Do you love me more than these?" What bothers him is the human or nonspiritual implication of this question: the human fashion of love of which there is more or less does not hold up before the risen One in whose presence these could be only an either/or of loving or not loving and in whose presence no man can boast of more. The only alternative to loving or not loving as I see it is an abstraction, what theologians call "docetic." Contrary to that I say simply that where there is love the heart is always more or less filled, there are always degrees. And when Peter gives us to understand that there is no part of him that does not share in this love he is talking about this qualitative business of more or less. That Jesus requires or presumes it here I take to be quite human, as a sign that he is talking on our level and perceives things "just as we do."

When the pietists say they love Jesus or that we must make the Lord Jesus dear to us then that may be somewhat compromised in a theological context (sometimes but not always). In principle something essential is being said that to take earnestly would do us so-called Protestants only good. For a certain rationality of our thought and a certain prevalence of theology over against faith express our poverty—that we often base our meaning on Christian ideas instead of on the person of Jesus, that we elevate the principle of love but not forget entirely the business of being enabled to love. Only the person of Jesus, its conduct and fate as it is vividly portrayed before our eyes, can free us to be able to worship to do this, not just our pious thinking and feeling and fantasy and imagination. The great saints and masters of meditation were quite aware of that.

Of course, this love does not stop at the human in Jesus. But it starts there. I cannot love the risen Lord if I did not first love the Creator of all in his transfiguration, whom Nicodemus visited at night, who helped the centurion of Capernaum, who blessed the children, wept for Jersusalem, and who forgave the executioner's henchmen beneath his cross.

Finally Jesus said to Peter that this love which legitimized his office of shepherd will cause him many difficult moments. But this is not really an idyll of love. A life in the Lord is separated from my natural life by a sharp division. "In those days," Jesus says, "You

were young and went where you wanted and did as you pleased,"
that is to say "when you were going," that is, you were not yet in
my service, you were your own master. But when you have grown
old and worn out and dedicated, then "others will lead you where
you do not want to go." Only he may expect to share in the life of
the risen Lord who dedicates himself and completely relinquishes
his own way.

The martyr experiences this in its extremest form. He gives himself unconditionally and is led where his natural inclination is not
to go. From Dietrich Bonhoeffer's letters—which he wrote before
the Gestapo murdered him—we know how much he hoped to go
on living so that he could serve to whom he wanted to belong. God
willed otherwise, however. The witness lives, however, and yet not
he, but Christ lives in him (Gal. 2:20). That is why he can be one
with him to the cross, into the torture of lostness, at any rate where
he does not want to go.

How can one survive this test? Certainly not by the strength of
a will that only fights against something, that is, the drive of self-
preservation, to conquer anxiety, yearning, and fear of total and
cold rejection. That would only be the resistance of a brave and
naked no against the deniers. With Jesus everything is positive. In
such borderline situations and in the hours of extreme inner tur-
moil I should see before my eyes the face of him whom I love.

I do not exist out of a no to me personally, nor to enemies or
functionaries, but because the joy of him whom I love is stronger
than the suffering to which I am called. This may be similar to the
inscription Count Zinzendorf read in the cross: "I did that for
you—What do you do for me?" "Peter, I have forgiven you your
denial; you know my feeling for you and I know you love me for
it. Will you deny me again?" To love means to be bound in heart
and therefore not to be able to betray one I love.

That is why Jesus is so positive. He puts something over and
against the power of darkness that I can love. And over this love
the power of darkness is powerless. For this reason Christ is also
present in the martyrdom of Peter. The witness does not simply
lose his life, he glorifies God with his sacrifice. He does that which
was done for him. He who loves never perishes in suffering. He
can praise God. The power to praise, however, points to that which

surpasses, that something more which suffering cannot overcome. In Gertrud von Le Fort's story, *The Last Ones on the Scaffold*, the nuns who sang hymns of praise at the executioner's block were just such loving people. They had a passion which was stronger than all torture. So even here it comes to that comparative which many theologians think is much too human and too unspiritual—stronger than all tortures, to love more than the others or than oneself before one received Jesus Christ.

CHAPTER 14

How Does One Cope with Unresolved Questions?

Now when John heard in prison about the deeds of the Christ, he sent word by his disciples and said to him, "Are you he who is to come, or shall we look for another?" And Jesus answered them, "Go, and tell John what you hear and see: the blind receive their sight and the lame walk, lepers are cleansed and the deaf hear, and the dead are raised up, and the poor have good news preached to them. And blessed is he who takes no offense at me."

Matt. 11:2–6

We understand this imprisoned John all too well. All of us rattle the bars in one way or another. Our worries surround us like so many bars.

There is the problem of growing crime and the escalation of terrorism. We worry that a couple of oil sheiks hold the habits of whole continents in their hands—and what questionable hands! We look anxiously at the hot spots in the Near East. And perhaps we are plagued by quite personal questions: illness, unemployment, increasing isolation, age, death. These are the encirclements that we cannot break out of or escape.

What people of spirit are there who on occasion are not beset by the Lord of sighs. If a righteous God were ruling the universe the world would have to look quite different. How can God permit this or that?

John in prison represents the situation of this desperate question rather exemplarily. He truly does not ask this question out of a theoretical interest in the puzzles of the universe (e.g., he is not

concerned with what one means by a theological technical term
such as "theodicy"). He does not ask from the detached perspective
of a disinterested observer but from disappointed involvement. He
has spent his life in God's cause; with word and deed he wanted
to prepare the way of the Messiah. Now his life's work seems to be
in jeopardy; he appears to be a beaten man.

Even his preaching in the wilderness, which seemed to be leading
to a turning point in the history of the world, seems now to be a
scrap of paper. Is he not a man who has been deceived, who on
his part has made himself guilty of deceiving those who believed
his word? Is he not a preacher of the wilderness who is now himself
sent off into the wilderness?

To understand these tattered thoughts one has to clarify John's
situation: he was proclaiming the arrival of God in his messianic
Messenger. He promised his hearers that his empowered Messenger would put an end to this world which had become impossible.
When he comes he will sweep the threshing floor (Matt. 3:12) and
he will tie the evidence to the torturers, bloodsuckers, etc. A storm
of renewal will then sweep over this rotten earth, for now there is
one who baptizes with fire and the Holy Spirit. A great day of
judgment will have done with this disappearing world of suffering
and injustice and begin to shape a new world that looks as though
God had designed it and not as something that man had warped.
But now John sits burned out and helpless in a prison cell. Has he
become a figure incredible to himself and to all men in what he
has promised? Why then is he tortured by the question: Have I
erred? Is this Jesus of Nazareth really the one I have seen in him
and whom thousands of listeners who trusted me have praised?

Let me go back just a step. If we do we see that John does actually
ask in this sense. And the little nuance in which he asks otherwise
is decisive here. He turns with his question directly to Jesus. It is
the same as later when Jesus himself, suffering the pain of the
cross, talks of being forsaken by God. Even there he does not cry
out in Golgotha's dark night: Where is God? I hang here in God-
forsaken emptiness; I have erred (similarly John). Paul lets the
"dead Christ" talk about the world building when he recants everything he proclaimed and calls sadly to man: "We are all orphans,
you and I. There is not a breast in which the heart of a father

beat." But the crucified One cries out his complaint to God himself about his sense of being left alone and speaks to him who threatens to throw him off the track: "My God, my God, why have you forsaken me?" So John does not say, "The Christ I preached to you is a fraud; and I, who fell for him, am a charlatan." No, Jesus himself should clarify this problem of doubt. That is why John puts the question to him: are you really the one for whom we wait or shall we look for another?

When in our doubt we appear to become insane because of God (and naturally of the figure of Jesus in which God draws near to us) we can only come farther when we put the question to God himself. The question, what it has to do with God, can be asked correctly only when we give it the "twist" of "Who are you?" Only then do we give him the chance of responding and of taking responsibility for his promise, if there is something to him. How does John phrase things in this way and give this address?

Although John is on the best—and most terrible—path of becoming insane because of Jesus, there is still something about this figure that will not let go. That is what tortures us. If we could only laugh at him and say: "You mad fool! How blind I was to fall for you!" Then it would be easier. When one can wash his hands of a former authority one is free to make a new beginning and look around for other guiding stars, wait for their appearance, and try it with them.

But even that is not the end for John. The magnet Jesus holds him firmly, even when he twists and turns. What holds him so firmly to Jesus?

While in prison John had heard something of the works of Jesus. That is, he heard about all those things that impressed people about Jesus and about which they began to speak. John may also have heard that Jesus helps, comforts, confers peace, and intervenes in need and sickness with his word of power, indeed, that he himself still seeks them in love and stays close to them even though they reject him. And it is just because this makes an impression on John and fascinates him that he is so tortured. It just increases the perplexity as to why this power and love are so ineffective in him and leave him to sit helplessly in his dark hole.

For this reason he finally turns to the Lord himself with his question-message: Who are you? I cannot shake myself loose from you. And yet I must ask you if you are really the one for whom we wait or shall we look for other saviors and miracle workers; for shakers and doers and revolutionaries who turn the world upside down.

I can imagine that concerns us because similar questions also move us. No one who has met Jesus ever gets entirely away from him. Even the greatest antichrists and atheists—from Nietzsche down to our day—testify to their respect for Christ. Nietzsche thought Jesus was the only Christian who ever was. And Alfred Rosenberg, the Nazi zealot against homosexuals, laid a great deal of value on the fact that he had never said anything derogatory about Jesus of Nazareth. Finally, Milan Machovec, the atheist philosopher, admits what a depth of humanity had been opened through Jesus. Even they could not tear themselves away from Jesus any more than could John as he sat in prison. But most of them do not think that Jesus has the final, saving word; rather, that that word belongs to the great doers and changers of the world. We would have to be looking for their kind even if every now and again we had to cast an admiring glance in the direction of the likeness of Jesus of Nazareth.

What is Jesus' reply to this moved and moving question of a tortured soul? On his answer depends the fate of a human being, indeed, of us all.

At first glance, the answer appears to be a rather disappointing one: "Tell John what you hear and see: the blind see, the dead are raised, and the poor have the gospel preached to them." John does not learn any more than what he already knew or had heard by the grapevine. He simply receives a report about what Jesus is doing. But that is just what raised the tortured question in him. Now his question comes back to him like an echo. How enigmatic it all is. What is behind it?

Further, something negative is important. He does not give a direct answer and he does not say outright: "Yes, I am he who is to come; I am God's Messiah. You need not look for another." Nor does he come to John with such titles as Messiah, Christ, Son of God, etc. What good would that do?

How often have we said in the course of penetrating conversations: "I just cannot believe this business about Jesus being God's Son or any of the other dogmas people have attached to his person.

I see him as a mortal man of tremendous power and purity (so that I almost again understand that he has been elevated to divinity). If I have to go along with this, what kind of Christian am I?" In such instances would there have been any sense in telling the questioner about the doctrine of Christ's two natures—human and divine—or try to explain the depths of the doctrine of the Trinity? Faith never begins at the top with such ideas as that of the Trinity or of predestination. Rather, faith begins down below where we become acquainted with the facts of this singularly unique life. It certainly does no harm to recognize simply and honestly how one permits the biography of a great man to work on one without dogmatic presuppositions.

This is the way Jesus acts in his answer. He refers to his mighty deeds in which the hopes are fulfilled that are mentioned in the word of the prophet (Isa. 35:5f.; 28:18f.; 61:1).

But there again we encounter disappointment because we obviously are not delivered out of our dead-end street. Of what help is it to us to point to his miracles? Even if it meant something to John to do that, what can it mean to us? Gotthold Lessing struggled with this problem when he saw himself pushed to a skeptical assertion: Another kind are the miracles which I myself experience. Another kind are those of which I only hear, which others claim to have experienced. Can miracles and displays of power legitimate anything when I only hear about them in roundabout ways, hearsay, etc., and therefore they are under suspicion of being nothing but legends? Even for the contemporaries of Jesus, who saw his acts with their own eyes, miracles could not overcome this problem. Miracles are problematic even for the eyewitnesses—not in the same sense that their supernaturalism must be put in doubt and explains them naturally, but in the sense that the question remains open as to what kind of power is at work here: that of God or that of Beelzebub (Matt. 12:2, 4ff.; 21:33). Miracles do not lead from faith to seeing and thus to security and conviction attained by having seen. Seeing with one's own eyes is as helpless against unbelief as is the word. It does not relieve us of doubt or decision. Miracles refer us—and Jesus' contemporaries—to the person of the One who performs miracles. The decisions are made on that basis only.

Strictly speaking, Jesus' reply to John does not point to miracles but to himself, to the mercy inherent in his helping deeds. Jesus points only to the fact that he is there for the least of us. He demonstrates by his actions that it is not a matter of the great God who is above all earthly matters, it is a matter of his descent to us, his love for us which is so great that he takes upon himself the fate of one who is tortured. He points to the love which breaks through the devilish principle of "as you do to me so I do to you." He confesses himself to be the messenger of joy who still calls into depths so deep that they cannot possibly escape God's presence and coming.

Our decision rests on him and his person. He is the secret theme of his miracles. Therefore his miracles are not overwhelming public displays of his power before which we must yield. On the contrary, they share in Jesus' weakness. Instead of being overwhelmed by them we can take offense at these miracles. The barrier remains. Only in this way can we understand what Jesus meant when he said "Blessed is he who [despite these wondrous deeds] takes no offense at me."

How does Jesus present himself in his miracles and message to John? How did he want to come to John and to us?

The question whether I can trust Jesus can be answered only by putting that person to the test on the most varied levels of life. And then, too, I must be convinced that what Jesus says is convincing. I must hear and be moved by what he says in the Sermon on the Mount where he uncovers the depths of a person and at the same time shows how one can find his way to another path to love and trust. I must let myself be worked on as Jesus was by the children, by a pressured mother, by the thoughtful Nicodemus or a seeker such as the rich young ruler.

Moreover, a great deal depends on making clear what kind of words he speaks. He does not simply docetize or fashion out a kind of system. But he always has a word that fulfills itself, that can tear up a life and make a fool of death. So he does not give a palsied person a lecture on the relationship of guilt, punishment, and forgiveness but tears up his bill, reduces his debt and opens up to him a new, freed life (Mark 2:1–12; cf. Col. 2:14). His Word completes the miracle of forgiveness and healing.

Thus with him Word and miracle are the same: Word is the miracle seen from within; miracle is the Word seen from without. One may call to mind the death passage in Paul Gerhardt's passion hymn, "O Sacred Head Now Wounded," which says: "And at the time I'm dying, O Lord, stay by my side." This line means more than that the Lord will call down words of consolation or wisdom concerning man's mortality. This line means much more—that dying in fact brings about a change. But the Lord does not let me fall into nothingness, he is with me. He stands with me in life and when I die he supports my falling head with his hand. Even at our death he speaks a word that makes our death a going home, a taking away of our loneliness.

But to win confidence a great deal more has to happen: I must ascertain if he keeps his word and if his life is congruent with his words. We watch how he hangs on the cross and ask ourselves if he is really honest about the things he says about loving and for-giving one's enemy. Only when we hear him, in the midst of his suffering, pray for his executioners does his commandment to love our enemies win any validity from us who at first turned a deaf ear to it.

I said that if you want to trust another you have to put him to the test, not just observe him—for example, really to cast my con-cerns on him, let them become his, and not worry about them anymore. What could happen? Would he be a washout or is he right? We have to try him and see.

Or suppose we really would try to get along with someone with whom we find getting along with very difficult. What will come of that? Or if we are ridiculed and vilified, will we experience the miracle of a new relationship? And even if everything goes wrong, do we not get closer to our neighbor and have a sense of joy in sharing his bearing of the cross? We have to try him. No one can come to a decision about him who has not put him and his way to the test.

Confidence comes only from trial and testing. Only he who dares such an experiment can experience who he is. Confidence is always such a risk. Jesus himself said that people would take offense at him. The recommendation that we put him to the test carries no guarantee that we will come to faith. Testing is a method. Here we can only risk something—but in the shadow of a promise—that God will not cast out one who seeks him with all his heart (see Jer. 29:13).

He who has found and experienced that Jesus really is the one who was to come and that we do not wait for another will have to say this: it was not the seeking of my heart that led to success; nor hardheadedness that brought me to peace. No—he has *given* me all that. He came to me! I would not even have sought him if he had not found me beforehand—and everything is true that he had promised me no matter how much of an adventure it sounded like for a beginner in faith.

Is the John in us willing to take the risk of bringing to Jesus his own lameness, blindness, inconsolable poverty, in order to be made new and happy by him and give him the opportunity of showing himself as the mighty Savior in our life?

Everything depends on that. That we can be free even in chains and comforted in the deepest depths. Then we would experience the arrival in our life that makes everything new and we would know at once what life can be.

CHAPTER 15

A Fire That Is
Not Consumed

And the angel of the Lord appeared to him in a flame
of fire out of the midst of a bush; and he looked, and lo,
the bush was burning, yet it was not consumed. And Moses
said, "I will turn aside and see this great sight, why the
bush is not burnt." When the Lord saw that he turned
aside to see, God called to him out of the bush, "Moses,
Moses!" And he said, "Here am I." Then he said, "Do not
come near; put off your shoes from your feet, for the
place on which you are standing is holy ground." And he
said, "I am the God of your father, the God of Abraham,
the God of Isaac, and the God of Jacob." And Moses hid
his face, for he was afraid to look at God.

Exod. 3:2–6

How easily the name of God falls from our lips. Especially to curse!
The hammer hits our finger! Or we do something stupid. Then it
is goddamn this, or oh, God, that!

What does all this mean when statistics tell us that 90 percent of
the people believe in God? What does it mean that there is a supreme being of which we can speak?

This assumption does not mean that I have to change anything
in my life. I have the same problems I would have had without
them. My apathy about starving children in India remains untouched; likewise the relationship to my colleague with whom I can
begin nothing. Here God has very little status.

For the people who have truly experienced God and then have
lived with him, God has a deep inroad into their lives. He does not

serve them as a religious enlightenment of their lives but encounters them as a fright (for a supreme being in his pallor of thought is never able to shine forth)—even in the joy of Christmas night the entire heaven is filled with the terror of the shepherds: "They were sore afraid." And Peter after his miraculous catch of fish is not exuberant with his catch but says, full of terror, "Depart from me, for I am a sinful man" (Luke 5:8). The majesty of Jesus humbled him in its strange greatness. One may think of Luther who left the altar with dispatch because he could not stand the holiness of God and the depth of his distance. The young monk knew that God wanted his life. But first it seemed God wanted to take him by his life.

It is the same here with Moses: God lives in a fiery zone and the fiery heat makes it impossible to draw near him safely. God lives in a light that no man can approach (1 Tim. 6:16). God can encounter us in terror—at least we take him seriously and come to terms with him: if we experienced from him only good, etc., as we know it, if he acted human in our mind then we would be snugly close and there would be no fear from him. But is this the way he deals with us? Thousands of people die in earthquakes in Japan and Pakistan; airliners crash with pious pilgrims on board; children are set upon by sexual deviates. How strange and puzzling God is! When Father Bodelschwingh lost his four children one after the other—in those days there were no antibiotics—he said: "Now I understand how hard God can be." Is he not hidden in the thorn bush to which one cannot draw nigh?

Little wonder then that one turns aside from this God and finds it more bearable to accept accidents and blind fate. At least one is spared the horror show of having to deal with a sadistic God. Nor is it astonishing that one flees off into junk novels where at the end scoundrels get their due or in utopian dreams in which a classless and just society rules the last act of earth's drama.

Now the question asserts itself if we Christians can bring about the experience of strangeness of God if we remain close to the innermost basis of our being. Could it not be that in their experience of terror Luther and Bodelschwingh lost this basis for a moment and fell into a crisis? Or, to put it another way, have the experiences of God changed since Jesus came among us? In him God is completely with us in human form. He does not stay away from us but accepts us and opens to us his Fatherly heart. He is with us in a man, a human being, who weeps with those who mourn and laughs with those who rejoice, to whom nothing that is human is foreign and who is human as we are. Is this not the divine secret of God which lies behind the burning bush?

Theology has always concerned itself with the historical Jesus. And not infrequently it did so with the intent of finding a familiar human figure and in that figure finding the secret of God and the experience of him. But it is significant to note that the Jesus we find with historical means and identify with them has something unfriendly about him, something brusque. He just cannot be laid hold of. Any many searchers collapse in their own skepticism and conclude that it is all a matter of a fire of straw, a blown-up mentality.

Is not this question of the historical Jesus a questionable business if one hopes to gain a solution to a puzzle of revelation? That is supposed to fit the Lord in tailored clothes behind the burning bush after one has put on asbestos gloves with the help of philological skills (of a *Formgeschichte* and hermeneutical kind) so as not to get any blisters? That is supposed to fit Jesus so you can say that this is the historic Jesus the way he really was? We have prepared him from all the coatings and legends and fantasies and now you can see for yourself what there is to him.

In reality the encounter with the historic Jesus is very much like Moses' encounter with God. God did not say to Moses as he stared at the burning bush which was not consumed something like: Put off your asbestos gloves, now you have me! Rather he says take off your shoes and do not come too close. And just as God has something about him which drives us away, so does Jesus as far as these people who approached him with a curiosity, so Jesus is separated from us by a great distance.

Perhaps no one has shown this protective zone as dramatically as Albert Schweitzer in his famous research on the history of the life of Jesus. When one raises up the last level of covering congregational theologies with the help of historical aids one discovers not the expected Savior figure or even a simple human being of his time, but rather an apocalyptic figure who escapes us, a really foreign figure that escapes us. The fiery border of the rosebush is more rejecting and inpenetrable than ever.

This is how it seems to be in this burning bush scene: the closer we get to it the more the fright grows, the alienness. Or . . . ?

In what can the reason lie that God has something terrifying here for Moses?

We get a first answer when we see that Moses is called by his name. Moses! He sees that he is known. He is the one who is meant. He knows he must stand still and cannot evade the call. God is at the boundaries of his life.

It is much simpler to mouth the expression "Supreme Being," for such a being does not know our name. It is completely different when I must reply to my name and say "Here I am."

With God every story has to begin with this necessity of giving an answer. I realize that it is I who is meant and recognized (1 Cor. 13:12). With God I have to do something. Without doing anything I am involved only with my own imagination. How many men of God have spoken of that because they were struck by a word— actually only a single word—as though by a bullet or an arrow, etc. So a word can lead one into the open: "Fear not; I am with thee." That too, grips my life and lays hold of me and obligates me.

Who is it who speaks out of the burning bush?

And who is this God who calls us by name and takes us by the hand? Who is it who speaks to us from the burning bush? Even Moses asks and wants to know with whom he is dealing. In the report following our passage God appoints Moses to negotiate Israel's exodus with the great pharaoh and appoints him to the leading role in this historic task. Moses declined at first. "Who am I that I should go to Pharaoh and lead the children of Israel out of Egypt?" And from the burning bush comes the answer which sweeps away all hesitation and fear: "I will be with you."

But this steeling of the backbone is of no avail, for who is this I who will be with me? Some unidentified confederate of unknown power? And if this I makes an impression—obviously a great impression—there is still the question of how he makes the experience of this call credible and clear. If he said that this was the God of your fathers who spoke out of the burning bush and has

sent me to you so that I can take charge in his name and with his
approval of your emanicipation, then we will ask: Who then was
this God who negotiated such dreadful things with you? Was it
really the God of our fathers? What was his name? What kind of
answer will he give? He had nothing in his hand; he did not know
his name. How could he legitimate his call and make it credible.
But God does not give the desired answer. He refuses to give his
name. Why?

Historically it can be explained why God does not want to be
included in the ranks of the other gods that have a name. Nor does
he, like them, want to be parables or the like of what is in heaven
or on earth or in the water beneath the earth (Exod. 20:4). He
keeps his distance from all of these. That is why he refuses to have
a name that turns up in the inventory of deities.

Time and again we experience how dangerous it is to manipulate
the name of God. How empty and hollow when we stand with all
such names and titles at the ready. "Christ," we say, "is the Son of
God." But what is it we are saying?

We have covered him with dogmatic formulas, the etiquette of
tradition. Once again we have put on the asbestos gloves so we do
not feel the heat and can deal with God's name like so many everyday objects which we keep in our drawers and on our shelves.
Behind all of these slick words and sounds there yawns again the
great emptiness. Our listeners, to whom we come with all our names
and titles, usually react with the question: "So what?" They do not
feel as though they are called by name. Such sermons wear themselves out in the acoustics.

Do not many of our worship services degenerate into liturgical
ceremonialism and duty-doing because we do not hear what this
burning bush has to say to us that really concerns us and strikes
home with us.

What happens in our story when Moses knows that he is called
by his name and struck to the quick?

Even though God refuses to give his name he nonetheless makes
himself known to Moses in a very unique way. He introduces himself as "the God of Abraham, Isaac, and Jacob," as the God of their
fathers. And then he calls himself "Jahwe." Actually that is not a
name but shorthand for a promise which in full reads: "I am what

I am, and will be what I will be." That sounds like some kind of puzzle word. The salvatory act of the Old Testament has become much clearer so far as what that meant and what mission was assigned to Moses with God's introduction of himself, "If you want to know who I am—this word Jehovah says—then stop asking about my name or my metaphysical presence. Even more, look at how I dealt with your fathers, how I called them, judged them, had grace upon them and led them in wonderful ways. Who am I, you ask? I am never there for you in my naked majesty. I am always in something and you find me only in some disguise in which I permit myself to be found. Here I am in a fiery bush which burns but is not consumed. In the case of the fathers—Abraham, Isaac, and Jacob—I was concealed in a variety of life confrontations and circumstances. Look! Listen to how I called them: Adam, where are you (or even Cain!)? And then in his own way each one must give answer: Here I am. In these encounters, in the stories of my people and of humankind in general—this is where you will find me and know me and experience who I am."

With the statement "I shall be what I shall be," God wants to say something like this: I will reveal myself henceforth in the act of saving, in what I permit to happen to you. That is where I show you with whom it is you have to deal. "I shall be what I shall be." And he will be faithful, as he was with Abraham, Isaac, and Jacob.

If the name were intended as some kind of concept which conveyed the essence of God, then we would know all about him once and for all. I would have him in my power just by having his name. The old fairy tales carry something of this idea. In it we have something of how we try to master and lock God up in our little concept-houses when we give God names: by God we understand that which is good or the moral world order, world reason. We define him by norms produced by human intellect and judge him by criteria which we have set up. If he does not meet these criteria, for example, what we consider to be good or sensible, then he has failed our examination. We smile at him as at an outdated illusion from which we turn aside when we want to make a picture of the world that is more to our liking.

Here we touch upon the deepest background of that refusal to give his name reported in the story of the burning bush: God evades our grasp that seeks by means of names and concepts to win control over him and to incorporate him in our human conceptions. No, we do not experience the name. We do not know specifically and once and for all everything about him, as we do, for example, in knowing for sure and all time that two times two is four. We just cannot have God in black-and-white and stick him in *our* pocket. His self-identification with the puzzle word, "I will be what I shall be," refers only to him whom it concerns, who embraces us in his action and in what he is.

We experience who he is when we have dealings with him and admit him into our hearts. Then in all change and puzzlement we will realize that he is faithful and that in grace and judgment we encounter the same identity of God.

The name "Jahwe" holds one fact: namely, the assurance that God's giving of himself will follow in any case. Therefore we can go in trust with God toward our future and be certain that all things are in his power. For this reason the term "Jahwe" is probably better interpreted to mean "I will be there for you and you will have occasion to take note." The existence of God meant in the designation is not being in itself (as in the case of the God of the philosophers) but a being for us.

Two points need to be mentioned yet. First, that bush burned but it was not consumed.

It burned. The figure of fire is always used to designate the pressure of God and the working of his Spirit. The same is true of the Pentecost story (Acts 2). Faith has something enflaming about it. Witnesses are people who have been caught up, enflamed. The stammering speech in tongues (1 Corinthians 14) may be an extreme form of this being caught up. Even more understated is the more questionable and traditionally more polished style of many of our church hymns. Have not the Negro spirituals given us a far more appropriate picture of what it means to be caught up by the Spirit? Nowadays something is beginning to show itself in the music of younger Christians. There is something hopeful about that and it demands patience to carry on calculated experimentation.

Finally, the bush is not consumed. The fire which burned was a symbol for the Being of God, not of the piety of people and their emotional condition.

Human enthusiasms are fires of straw. Fireworks fizzle out. They do not give the light we need in "death's dark vale." But when the torch of faith has been thrown into our hearts by God it cannot be extinguished and reduced to dead ash. On the contrary, it glows hotter and more brightly. We never grow above the Word that enkindles this flame within us; we grow more deeply into it. How little of our youthful dreams survive when we grow older; how much that we experience wears itself out and becomes boring. The fire of faith burns brightly ahead of us and leads to new surprises. And when an aged man has finally experienced all that is to be experienced in this life and has run life's sole so that its heels are worn out, he stands before what is not exhausted or consumed and each day confers upon him the miracle of new discoveries.

Whoever examines a story with the incarnate Word, with Jesus Christ, is led from one clarity to another. The older he gets the more will occur to him. And the fullness of the as-yet-undiscovered remnant will let him wait (to use Søren Kierkegaard's grave inscription) for the eternity in which he can always and forever speak with Jesus in order to learn the fullness of truth from him. The glory of Jesus does not consume itself. Jesus' high priestly prayer (John 17) in which he shines forth as the countenance of God is something of which we never learn enough. This burning bush never extinguishes itself.

PART FOUR

GOD'S MYSTERY
IN THE FORM
OF JESUS

CHAPTER 16

The Adventure of Discipleship

The seventy returned with joy, saying, "Lord, even the demons are subject to us in your name!" And he said to them, "I saw Satan fall like lightning from heaven. Behold, I have given you authority to tread upon serpents and scorpions, and over all the power of the enemy; and nothing shall hurt you. Nevertheless do not rejoice in this, that the spirits are subject to you; but rejoice that your names are written in heaven."

In that same hour he rejoiced in the Holy Spirit and said, "I thank thee, Father, Lord of heaven and earth, that thou hast hidden these things from the wise and understanding and revealed them to babes; yea, Father, for such was thy gracious will. All things have been delivered to me by my Father; and no one knows who the Son is except the Father, or who the Father is except the Son and any one to whom the Son chooses to reveal him."

Then turning to the disciples he said privately, "Blessed are the eyes which see what you see! For I tell you that many prophets and kings desired to see what you see, and did not see it, and to hear what you hear, and did not hear it."

Luke 10:17–24

First Meditation
The Demonic Powers:
Gray Zones Between Faith and Superstition

The theme under consideration here is Satan and the demonic powers. Immediately we think about those dreary old mansions with creaking boards and stairways. One can almost see the ghosts and goblins hovering about. We can even imagine an encounter or two with devils. We moderns have our working buildings of steel and concrete. Our hospitals, clinics, and laboratories are made of glazed tile and are lighted with neon lights with the brightness of day. There are no dark corners or mysterious actions. That is why we recall coming from such quarters when suddenly the talk here is about Satan, of a physical God with us.

Or on the stage, what would Faust be without Mephistopheles? We are not dealing with a simple superstition here but have the feeling that a truth of life, which we sense is a deep one, is pressing to the fore. A man like Faust can accomplish great things, but only in league with the forces of evil—that gives us pause to think.

Did we not experience something of the kind with Hitler? And his key aide, Albert Speer, speaks of this specifically in his memoirs, how the prospect of gigantic building programs that would last for thousands of years to come and of lasting time proved to be more than he could withstand so that the pact with the devil Hitler was not too high a price for him to pay for such fame.

In his *Epimenides*, Goethe spoke of that successful world conqueror Napoleon Bonaparte as a man in league with the powers of darkness which ultimately cast him down just as they had raised him up.

But can we accept the idea of the devil of whom Luke speaks in his gospel? What can we make of that, or is this a piece of superstition from a prerational time?

Perhaps it would be good before making any other observations to say something by way of orientation. The Bible is remarkably reluctant—in fact, it is totally disinterested—in all speculation about the manner and existence of the powers of darkness. The Bible is satisfied to say what can be seen of the workings of these powers: for example, how people lose control over themselves, become alienated or come under the influence of some power outside themselves. So they are shaken by the spirit of worry and all attempts to become clear and rational about nothingness is of no help. The spirit of worry, anxiety, and depression continues to shake them. It is like when a person takes the first step to winning power, then in the next instance is freely gripped by the intoxication of power which abducts him to that place where he originally did not want to go.

The Bible deals with the effects of the powers of darkness not only for its own part, at least not in the sense that it speculates about those powers' nature and origin. For example, the Bible gives no answer to the question of how evil came into the world and who or what the serpent brought into paradise. This reluctance is concerned not only with the Devil but even with Christ himself. There is no speculation about the divine and human natures of the Lord and how the two are related to each other. In any case there are questions that are hidden throughout the gospels; but they are not treated and answered, only passed over. Only later generations discovered these questions and beat their heads together over them. The Bible is concerned exclusively with what Christ does. We discussed that in a previous meditation (unresolved questions) and are reminded that when John the Baptist, who had announced his coming, sat doubting in prison and questioned who this Jesus of Nazareth might be, if he really were the king who was to come on that last day or whether they should wait for another, Jesus gave John a message as to what he is doing and leaves it to John to make sense of it.

At first glance our text has nothing to do with such thoughts. We sooner get the impression of superstition which we today think we have overcome. Even today if we only speak of evil, bad—not to mention demons—people make an ugly face. Can we not explain all that rationally? A criminal—for example, a Charles Manson, who murdered an entire group of people in Hollywood—is more possessed by the devil than he is a devil in human form. O no! Society is at fault because society unleashed aggressive drives in such people. One does not need exorcism, rather, social therapy programs are needed. Behind the glaring contradictions of rich and poor, exploiters and exploited does there stand some satanic power? No! Only false structures are responsible for this disorientation. One can define the errors exactly. Here it is a matter of accounting, not mysticism. Was not the famous murderer of boys, Juergen Bartsch, under a similar demonic power? Or was it not rather a case of genes and hormones. The predominance of perverse drives can, in our day, be controlled by drugs and psychotherapy and surgical operations—at least to a large extent.

In our day there is a housing shortage for the devil. He cannot find housing anywhere. One hardly finds a spot for the inexplicable where he can move in before that space is occupied by quite natural matters of psychology, sociology, or physiology. If the devil is driven out of our consciousness but not out of us, then we simply cannot understand the joy of the disciples at having received antidemonic power. One no longer knows why; who needs a Savior who can crush the forces of evil?

A bit of caution is advised. We should take the advice of Goethe who, though he was not a church Christian knew something about the devil (and indirectly something about God), when he said: "Plain folks wouldn't recognize the devil even if he had them by the throat." Somewhere Goethe says the devil does his best so as not to be recognized, but yet to be effective; that "though the devil has long ago been consigned to the fable book, men are no better off: they have lost the Evil One but have kept the evil ones!"

When he wrote that Goethe must have had in mind the biblical story of the Fall, for even in the Garden of Eden the devil did not reveal his identity. Elsewhere we have noted how the devil behaved in an entirely undevilish way and even sought to have a serious theological conversation with Eve about whether God could have said a certain thing and about how un-Godlike it was of God to declare a part of his own creation—the tree in the middle of his garden—as off-limits and not to be touched.

If that is how things are, then a very weighty question asserts itself: If we deny the satanic element, could it be that we fall victim to this strategy of evil? Could it not be that the devil wishes to delude us into thinking that in the rational brightness of self-conscious modern man the devil has completely disappeared? Perhaps we will see in our text a little more clearly; and perhaps afterward we will be a bit less cocksure of ourselves.

Goethe, whom we have quoted before, also once said that in the last analysis history is a struggle between faith and unbelief. And Karl Marx argued the thesis that history is a story of class struggle. Others speak of history as a struggle between good and evil. Still others stress what it is that the struggle is against: against unjust structures, slavery, and exploitation, against hunger and population explosion. In any case we always stand before an example of struggle. And we are always struggling against some evil and destructive power. What is this evil power? That is the question.

Jesus' followers have experienced not only in connection with this first commissioning but with the entire dramatic history of mission throughout the ages that the faith has to struggle against all manner of foes and circumstances and that the ·blood of the martyrs has shown the way of the struggle. The disciples are soldiers of Christ who must be led on the battlefield. They must be brave. And in every situation they face, the "old bitter foe" is recognizable as our opponent. The devil is always on the loose in this world. Reinhold Schneider may have had this observation in mind when, during World War II, he expressed his skepticism about the ability of any mortal (he meant Hitler) to carry anything through to completion and said:

> Men of action will never compel heaven;
> What they negate, will divide yet
> once again;
> What they renew,
> Will grow old overnight

What he may have meant by that perhaps becomes clear when we think of the word "devil" ("one who brings confusion"). There is a power to confuse that comes into play everywhere where human beings bring their power to reason to bear. Let me show what I mean with a couple of illustrations from everyday life. Two people—perhaps a married couple—can no longer get along. A ridiculous little quirk (perhaps one makes annoying noises while chewing, or the other slurps his or her soup) on the part of one more and more gets on the nerves of the other. The one reacts in increasing frustration at the other until a rational resolution of their differences is impossible. Both of them are under a kind of spell, as it were.

Is this talk of a spell just an employment of the means of psychology to throw some light on such events? Does such a term clarify the whole business?

A personal experience illustrates what this spell means. Independently of each other two of my students told me that in 1945 they once had greeted one of my colleagues, a respected university professor, with "Grüss Gott," a traditional greeting. The professor replied curtly, "You mean Heil Hitler!" Now, I knew this particular professor was a member of the Nazi party although he later emphasized that his membership was just a matter of formality, that in fact he was not in sympathy with the Nazis and had actually—although secretly—supported the Resistance. I considered it my duty to confront him openly about his conduct toward these students (I knew both of them and trusted their reliability). To my astonishment he made no bones about his insistence upon the Nazi greeting. In fact, he was incensed about this alleged defamation by the students. Now, I had known this man for a number of years as a faculty colleague—well enough to know that he was not going to put up some kind of defense and tell me a lie. What happened showed me what the Bible meant by the power of the demonic. During the Hitler years an alien spirit had captivated him. This spirit had so taken hold of him that he identified with the party and its creed to the extent that in that spirit's name he believed he was speaking in his own name. When the collapse came in 1945 the ideological fascination was gone. Now that he was entirely alone and had found his true identity he could not remember that he had said this or that. It was not his own spirit but an alien spirit that had spoken out of him. His self-respect told him to say he was not the one who had said the offensive greeting. But his conscience insisted that he had.

Psychoanalysts like to speak here of "suppression." Fine! I have nothing against that. But what does that mean? What does that say about the power that pushes itself ahead and that is later suppressed? To what extent is the relationship between an alien spirit and a spirit which alienates us from our own identity clarified? I think it is more appropriate and meaningful and more in a New Testament sense to speak of a possession, that is, of a power which holds us. The *diablos* or devil confuses what is us with what is strange and foreign and alien.

One final example. Someone is hurting very badly from deep and disturbing anxieties. Dear and understanding friends talk with him and try to reason with him and make it clear that there is no reason for his concerns, only secret ones nesting in hidden anxieties that turn themselves into a series of pictures projected on the walls of his life. He trembles before fire and water and dagger and poison and he is constantly lamenting what he never lost. (Does he not at least in part have fear of atomic warfare?) But all their well-meaning words bear no fruit, even when the tortured person has some kind of rational insight. It is as though some power were taking hold from behind, but never from in front and in the open. The gospel speaks of a spirit of worry that overwhelms such a person.

Again we assume that we can help such people by means of psychoanalysis, by reference to dreams of youth, and thus take away this alien spirit and restore unharmed his person again. What is finally achieved before the end may be some improvement. The relationship of one's own person to the alien spirit is not clarified as to its secret and the person who has been liberated as to his own identity stands now before new problems. What should he do with this person of his own that he has won? Are not people thus cured unbearably alone? Do they not need physicians of the soul who will say something to them about the basis, goal, and meaning of their own being? That is exactly where the problem of the foreign or alien spirit that comes from another side must come under discussion.

So we are constantly involved in discussion. We feel driven to do something out of our confusion, for example, in order to make the world better, help to make it less a source of conflicts, and to defuse aggressive drives so that we can overcome social injustices. The natural man always perceives that as his sole mission. So he hears these imperatives called out to him: If you want to live in an up-to-date way you must have a brave heart. (But where do I get a brave heart and what good does it do me if the power of confusion does not look me in the face?) And in the face of the reality of guilt there is this command: Do what is right and fear no man! (But who can do that? Is there some power in us which, despite all good intentions never lets this happen?) Slogans such as "have a cheerful disposition" are commonplace panaceas against anxiety. But how can I conjure up such a disposition when the power of melancholy holds sway over me?

Luther once said to come to Christ is like coming out of the dark house of this life into the bright sunlight of Christ, like when one comes out of the realm of the dark power into the realm of the conqueror.

And that is exactly what the seventy disciples experienced when they were sent out in our text. They experienced what the power of evil experiences, that imprisonments, subjections, serfdoms, and possessions must give way where the conqueror of guilt, sorrow, and death comes into play. They tread on serpents and scorpions and were immune to their bite, and they also proclaimed the gospel not like a new world view as the wise and learned (Luke 10:21) would do, but they had an effective and powerful word at hand that changed people and tore their chains. Was that power of theirs suggestive or rhetorical? Was it their collective effect? Their bravery? No. Basically they did not accomplish anything. They established only something that had already been accomplished; they accomplished it only afterward. Why could they break the power of darkness? Because these powers already lay in the dust. The Master confirms this impression when he mentions that during their crusade he saw Satan fall from heaven like lightning. Because Christ is there the powers of darkness are overcome. They can do nothing to us when we call upon Christ's name. "He's judged; the deed is done; one little word o'erthrows him." "Ask ye who this may be [who has done this], Christ Jesus it is he." Christoph Blumhardt was one of those who performed what had already been done when, in the presence of Gottliebin Dittus, a victim of possession, he said: "We have seen for long enough now what the devil can do. Now let us see what Jesus Christ can do."

What, then, can he do and how does our relationship to the confusion-bringer (devil) change in Christ's sphere of influence?

There is an oft-mentioned spirit of worry. Jesus demands that we resist this (Matt. 6:25). But this struggle has a chance only because the evil spirit of worry and care has already been overwhelmed: the Father knows what we need. So he has taken that which concerns us to his own heart. Therefore the spirit of worry must yield step by step as we lay hold of his Fatherly concern and care.

There is the power of anxiety. But its source—the feeling that we are at the mercy of the incalculable—is stopped: Christ has indeed overcome the world (John 6:33). He who holds the fate of the world in his hands can also let peace enter into men's hearts so that anxiety has no more room. Who sees him coming across the waves no longer fears the threatening of the elements.

There is the power of guilt, the torture of the conscience. Our own struggle against guilt would be not only hopeless but ominous as well (as we saw earlier in the case of my teaching colleague). One can only be cramped in. If I fight alone with my conscience I am compelled to build up some form of defense. Since the coming of Jesus Christ who dares to accuse God's elect of anything? It is God who justifies (Rom. 8:33). That means God counts us as righteous regardless whence we come or what scars we bear. He sees in us the brothers of his son whom he has bought at a great price. That is why he accepts us and rejects the accuser. There is no longer anything that can come between him and us and separate us from him (Rom. 8:39). I no longer have to struggle against my bad conscience, no longer need to suppress it because it has lost its function as a power to separate and God no longer rejects a loaded conscience that calls upon the name of Jesus.

Luther once expressed this in a magnificent wordplay: first God is my accuser, my conscience, my defender. But then it comes to a radical substitution of fronts: in the light of the gospel my conscience accuses me, for in this light it seems clearer than before— it is even more sensible—God is now my defender and defends me before the accusation of my conscience. The certificate of guilt is torn up and hung on the cross (Col. 2:14).

Finally there is the power of despair which would like to drive us mad because of God. Despair makes God's direction of the world appear impenetrable. Despair emphasizes (and mockingly) that the rascals and big shots always come out on top while the pious little fellow gets it in the neck (Psalm 73).

And yet, in spite of all the misery, all of the injustices which scream out, in spite of all the Auschwitzes and Buchenwalds, the faithful still raise up their songs of praise. How could they do it? Was it by a stretch of the effort of will. I believe it even if their victory was ever so razor thin. No! It was the risen Christ, the victory that had already taken place, which gave the sovereign certainty that all the paths of life, however painful and perplexing, find their end at the throne of God. They lived—and we live--under the promise that we do not yet understand what is happening to us, but we shall (John 13:7). To praise God means to see history from the vantage point of its end.

Everything we are supposed to do has its sense and reason in what has already taken place. We have only to accomplish that which God has already brought to pass. From this we see just how we Christians should be active and how we should be passive. We should do and act exactly as did those seventy disciples in our text. We have to sweat, labor, toil for the kingdom. We must put on the helmet of Michael and not his nightcap. We have to set our hands to all kinds of reforms and revolutionary changes. We can do all that unperturbed and in peace because Christ is risen and because the decision has taken place. It is not we who want to lay hold of Christ's hand and draw it around the world to christianize the continents. No! His arm has already stretched around the world and we follow after it.

Our text offers one final reference to the basis of our unperturbed certainty of this peace. Jesus tells his disciples that he was the one who gave them the power over serpents, scorpions, and the powers of possession and he adds immediately "Do not rejoice about that!" That is to say, do not rejoice that you have been preserved and how you have been preserved; rather rejoice for the supreme reason for your certainty: because your names are written in heaven (Luke 10:20).

What has become of the great names of this world that are chiseled in stone? They have become weatherworn. They are preserved in our memory as names from the past, but they designate no physical presence of the present. But where Jesus Christ has called us by our name, our name is transported into the presence of God, into a place to which no one has access and where no one may erase our name. Here that name is a living name forever, the name of someone who shares in eternity the life of his lord (1 Thess. 5:10).

All we can produce and make by ourselves is nothing but gold, silver, and precious stones, wood and straw. How much questionable stuff there is in our lives! On judgement day the fire will give light and what dross will it not consume (1 Cor. 3:11)! May it then be that we ourselves will be saved by fire (1 Cor. 3:15)? Our names will remain. This book is kept in fireproof storage. Even our faith is fickle. We cannot trust in it. We cannot rely on our faith no matter how great that faith is. It can hardly inspire us to prayer and all manner of doubt nibbles on it. I do not know if I believe, but I know in whom I believe.

So our faith may be weak and almost dead. But we live in God's memory. We are bought at a price. The name remains written. Nowhere are we told that God is continually occupied with erasing and rewriting. What he has written he has written. Whom he has accepted remains his. Our enduring value, the memory of which he carries in his heart, consists not of our functions and what we have earned but in the fact that we are (to use Paul Gerhardt's term), "Jesus' companions."

And finally we should not overlook the hidden reference to this story: we can hear out of this account of the seventy that they were amazed to the extent that their word was a word that accomplished something and above all what authority they had been given over all dangers and troops of Satan. They had never expected all that and saw themselves always facing new surprises.

No one, before he becomes a Christian and enters the ranks of discipleship of Jesus, can even guess what miracles await him. The discipleship of Jesus is something into which one must first jump to know what is involved. What is given to us by way of freedom, sovereignty, and whatever else may come to us (1 Kings 3:13; Matt. 6:33) will be clear to us not in calculable distance but only in actual discipleship itself. Who Christ really is and what we win with him is something we experience only when we dare to enter into a relationship with him. That is when the surprises begin. That is when the adventure begins.

Second Meditation
In Praise of the Simple of Heart

Immanuel Kant once defined "enlightenment" as a pronounced forward step of the human spirit, man's rising above his immaturity. Simplicity and immaturity do not mean that a person's I.Q. is too little for one to move under one's own steam, intellectually speaking. Kant is speaking about an immaturity that is one's own fault.

What does Kant mean by this? He means simply that people want to avoid responsibility; they want to avoid standing on their own two feet. It seems easier and less risky to be led by the nose by all kinds of authority: by the spirit of the times that tells one how and what to think; by the church; probably even by God. Yet many people do not want to claim the freedom to their own responsibility and decision. That is too risky and strenuous. They are inclined, as Jean Paul Sartre once put it, not to opt for freedom. So in an artificial way we have opted for immaturity.

In our text the simple of heart are praised and exalted over the wise and clever, even over the mature.

How are we to understand this Word of the Lord? Does he want an artificial reversion to the stage of naiveté? Is the Lord a foe of culture and progress? Or is his Word to be understood in another way?

First we must be clear about the context of this Word. The seventy disciples have just returned from a journey of faith and proclamation. The Word with which Jesus sent them out is breathtaking: "I send you out as sheep among wolves. Take neither purse nor knapsack nor shoes!"

But this adventure has the promise that the field is "white unto the harvest." And they may be sure that there will be a harvest, that they are working on the side of the Lord of the harvest, and that they will endure. For the first time they dare to make the experiment of striking out into the world in Jesus' name and of saying farewell to the security of the fellowship of the Lord's band of followers.

Now they return with glowing reports of what they have experienced. Their word was, as Luther put it, not only a word of instruction but also one by which to live, a word that hit home and gave many a new start. Theirs was a word accompanied by signs and wonders. Theirs was a word that made things happen. And as they went off into the unknown they realized that they were tools through which the Lord himself was at work in the affairs of men. Jesus himself saw the vision of Satan falling from heaven like a bolt of lightning. This vision marked the beginning of the new eon and the breaking of the demonic powers. The serpent no longer has power over us. Jesus has bruised its head and now he and his can tread on scorpions and serpents. Jesus himself stands between us and the great darkness. The Father has given him power over the forces of darkness.

Our text permits us to share a moment when Jesus and the Father are immersed in deep conversation. Scripture speaks of such a moment of solitude as rejoicing in the Spirit. Jesus was full of joy even though he was surrounded by darkness—a dark into which he would have to descend when he set out for Jerusalem and his final sorrows. Even then he spoke of his woe over Chorazin and Bethsaida and Capernaum, which wanted nothing to do with him. If the miracles which had taken place in those cities had happened in Tyre and Sidon those cities would have donned sackcloth and ashes and repented (Luke 10:13).

Here he is surrounded by pure blindness and resistance. He sees disappointment and rejection wherever he looks and goes. And before him lies Jerusalem which had slain the prophets of yore. He knows what awaits him there and what those who have the say have up their sleeves against him. The wise, the clever, the mighty are the ones who are most against him and they seal up all the cracks through which his light could shine.

It is the same today. Would humanity be any happier through enlightenment and technical progress? Are not the dreams which surround this idea long since played out? Is not youth, which someday will have to pay the consequences for what unleashes atomic and biological forces of progress, most anxious because of the dreadful ability of human ingenuity? Is not man, who expects to take over God's place and inaugurate an eighth day of creation, thrown into an anxiety of life, into senselessness? Those who are most powerful and intelligent have their special dangers, and the arrogance of many so-called intellectuals is one of the greatest of these dangers.

And how is it with the wise and clever among Jesus' followers, the ones we call theologians? Do not the theologians know full well that theology not only can help to make discipleship something that is lived, but that it can also sow seeds of confusion? Learned scholars fall prey to error and madness when they parade as gentlemen of faith and cite their wisdom as an authority over the Word of God. God's Scriptures remain sound only so long as they are clear about one thing: that God wants our love, a love that comes from our total heart and recognition (Matt. 22:27). Only he who loves puts his total existence at another's disposal.

Then one participates with his whole mental being, that is, intellectually. And this compels one to acknowledge whom one loves and how it happens that this One has won his heart. A healthy theology centers its thoughts on the object of its love. This is a love that goes beyond emotional stirrings, that assumes responsibility for its devotion and hope (1 Peter 3:15; cf. also Eph. 1:1, 8).

So love is totally committed to its cause. Otherwise love would put only the province of emotion at Jesus' disposal, thus making him only a regional Lord, while intellect goes its own and other ways. Even intellect belongs to the entirety of our own person which God wants to win to himself and make it the place of his presence.

How can intellect become better, a more "listening" intellect? Only by immersing itself ever anew in the gospel message which proclaims Jesus' salvation and tells us that in Jesus' sphere of influence the blind receive their sight, the lame walk, the lepers are made clean, the deaf hear, and the poor have gospel preached to them (Matt. 11:15).

Healthy theology is one which returns to the roots of faith. Such theology embraces intellectually what the simple spirit grasps in a more naive way—that Jesus gives us new life, that the old is passed away and that our hearts are filled with living hope.

Even if a theology is a most highly intellectual pursuit, it lives by referring constantly to the simplest thing that won us to faith. To try to evade the business of thought, theology, means that one cannot belong entirely to God, for one withholds a substantial part of his person from his Lord. That is why there are so many stiff-necked Christians. And no amount of orthodoxy or swallowing of dogmas can make them anything different.

There are many ways in which one can be unfaithful to Jesus. One can do it by being a self-righteous Pharisee who prizes his own thoughts more highly than the gospel which every simple heart understands. Luther put it this way when he said: "To make progress [in faith and knowledge] is nothing other than to start anew," that is, to return to the simplest thing that won us to faith. We can also reject discipleship by becoming mired in pious feelings and withholding all the powers of heart and mind and intellect.

A sound theology demands the severity of thinking and childlike faith that can unite a genius with one who is mentally handicapped in a common discipleship. I experienced this in my student days when I studied under the great theologian Rudolf Hermann at Greifswald. He had spent an entire semester lecturing on the many abstract and complex thoughts of great thinkers and he had not made it easy for his students. His final lecture closed with this observation: "Gentlemen, all that we have dealt with in these lectures has said nothing other than what the old children's hymn says so simply and beautifully:

> Jesus' blood and righteousness
> Clothes me in a radiant dress
> Which makes me fit, our God to meet
> Before his heavenly judgment seat.

Professor Hermann's great knowledge did not stand between him and discipleship.

Let me suggest an addition to Jesus' parable of the Soils (Luke 8:4–15): God's Word can be hindered by our own cleverness.

Who are the lowly in our text? They are the seventy who have just returned from their mission. In all lowliness they dared and did what they were sent out to do. They trusted his promises and those promises do not lie. Jesus' words, of which they were messengers, accomplished great deeds; they freed and healed and triumphed over all demonic powers.

What kind of people were they? Certainly no one took them seriously? Socially and educationally speaking they were underprivileged. An old rabbinical expression would call them the "scum of the earth."

Indeed they were nothing, and it is grotesque that Jesus should want to change the world with their like. Where were the movers and shakers, the people of influence (cf. 1 Cor. 1:20)? Such people are impressed only by what is intellectually appealing or by the sensationalism of miracles (1 Cor. 1:22). But here we have only paupers, simplicity, and what, for human eyes, is only the madness of the cross.

We, too, must ask who are the people who matter when we look at our worshiping congregations. Where are the intellectuals, the cultivated, the upper classes? And where are the working classes? Their absence oppressed us especially because it raises the question of what the church's message omits. We wonder what has become of God's cause when so often we see only little people, old folks, and not the kind of people who are creative and make things happen in life.

It is precisely here that we see that Jesus is absolutely other than we; moreover, in spite of all his closeness he still keeps a distance from us. He rejoices in the Spirit. The apparent insignificance of the little band of faithful does not discourage him. His intellect must still speak to him despite all the pessimistic diagnoses. Yet he rejoices in the Holy Spirit. He looks at these things with other than human eyes. The Spirit opens to him all perspectives of the coming rule of God. And the glow of this rule shines over these seventy people. He knows that God always resolves his battles with the holy remnant, or, as Luther put it, that God knows how to ride the lame horse and to carve rotten wood. There is nothing and no one whom God cannot use as his instrument.

How God equips and uses even the weakest of instruments in his service is seen over and over in God's people. I remember that back during the struggle against the Nazis one of our leading men was a pastor I knew well. Before that time he had been a nobody in the church. His theological education was rather minimal and he was not much of a speaker or preacher. Once, when he had to read before a large audience the manuscript of a significant theologian whom the Gestapo had forbidden to speak, he stammered and stuttered so much that no one could understand what he was reading. But this little nobody soon began to shine like a great light in deepest darkness. He was a man filled with zeal and confidence. To read reports of the things that he said in those days one finds nothing particularly outstanding. But as a rule God does not fight the decisive battles with outstanding people but rather with witnesses whom he has equipped with his Spirit and upon whom his countenance has shown so that people follow them as the Hebrews once followed the pillars of fire. God can ride even a crippled horse.

We see something·of this in the Soviet Union today. Here the church is in the catacombs. It preaches its message with great difficulty. To have one's children baptized is a test of courage. To confess one's faith openly means to jeopardize one's career. To conduct any kind of religious education is largely impossible, so it is the old grandmothers who light candles and pray before the icons and who teach the children what faith is and how to pray.

The grandmothers!! How often the church is ridiculed as a church of old women, a church that is dying, whose end is at hand. There seems to be no coming generation, and yet we see that again and again these old "Sarahs" bear new generations of faithful. They are not the powerful of this world. On the contrary, they symbolize total powerlessness. They are neither wise nor clever, they are the simple of heart who faithfully guard the seed of the eternal word and sow that seed in the hearts of the children.

Should we then hold intellect in contempt? Should we abolish it along with all culture itself as so much junk? Jesus did not feel that way. He himself once said we should be as "wise as serpents"; that we should count the cost in building a tower and exercise sobriety in counting the cost of discipleship. In other words, when we set out to do something, we should be certain that our potential is equal to the task (Luke 14:28–32). Jesus called that farmer who ultimately trusted his full barns and ignored his relationship to God not only godless but a fool because he did not know what was essential in life.

It is not hostility to reason and intellect that is meant by the praise of the simple of heart and spirit. Much more is meant by the use of one's will and ability. For it is clear (and the story of the rich young ruler is a classic example): everything that makes us rich and talented, everything that is ours in a tangible and intellectual sense—everything—can come between God and us and become an idol, a false god in which we can come to trust (as did the rich farmer). But at the very end our idols will forsake us, for there are no pockets in a shroud.

What kind of hands do we really have? Are they open and out-stretched so that we can receive in gratitude with them? Are they open because it is clear that we cannot grab and manipulate what-ever we please, but that we can only receive what is given to us? It is clear that every action, even the intended actions of our hands, is a gift and that the intellectual ability that stands behind these hands is a gift. Or are our hands clenched because they want to hold on to whatever they touch, idealogues that want to shape the world in their own image?

Whoever wants his name to be written in the book of life has to dare to be with Jesus. Only the Son knows the Father. Whoever is near him is near the Father. Whoever does his will becomes identified with him whose will is done. Whoever prays in the name of the Son is heard by the Father and his word is accompanied by God's wonders. Here all science and worldly wisdom have their limits. We may penetrate the tiniest or the vastest; we may even overcome the smallest and largest. But peace with God, in which we find the fulfillment of our lives, cannot be grabbed, it can only be granted. There is no other way.

So, then, Jesus is not a teacher of life's wisdom; he is God himself come to us in a love in which no suffering or despair is too deep, a love in which his majesty rules all things and can change all things. All of this he has given power over to the Son. That is why Jesus is subject to no human power. He is neither the totality of religious man nor a founder of a religion. We know from the history of thought and from church history how the world has always tried to make him fit into its schemes. Only he to whom he reveals himself can grasp who he is.

One who beholds what prophets and kings desired to see can only ask in astonishment: "Why is this happening to me? I am just one of these insignificant seventy people. We certainly are no elite. Indeed, we are perhaps of much less significance than many an atheist and agnostic!" The lines from Friedrich Hiller's hymn suggest the answer:

> God's mercy has befallen me
> Why and how
> I do not know
> It's naught but mercy
> nothing else . . .

When one loves, one does not count the cost. And where one experiences that of which Hiller wrote one certainly does not count the cost, one simply falls to one's knees in adoration and gives heartfelt thanks.

God has given all things to this one whom we call Lord. For that reason we can give everything over into his care and completely entrust to him that with which we cannot cope, what oppresses us with worry and overwhelms us with anxiety. Indeed, it is true— between us and that deepest of darkness there stands our Lord, Jesus Christ.

CHAPTER 17

Learning by Praying

Then the mother of the sons of Zebedee came up to him, with her sons, and kneeling before him she asked him for something. And he said to her, "What do you want?" She said to him, "Command that these two sons of mine may sit, one at your right hand and one at your left, in your kingdom." But Jesus answered, "You do not know what you are asking. Are you able to drink the cup that I am to drink?" They said to him, "We are able." He said to them, "You will drink my cup, but to sit at my right hand and at my left is not mine to grant, but it is for those for whom it has been prepared by my Father." And when the ten heard it, they were indignant at the two brothers. But Jesus called to them and said, "You know that the rulers of the Gentiles lord it over them, and their great men exercise authority over them. It shall not be so among you; but whoever would be great among you must be your servant, and whoever would be first among you must be your slave; even as the Son of man came not to be served but to serve, and to give his life as the ransom for many.

Matt. 20:20–28

Naturally mothers are pleased when their sons amount to something. Our text presents us with a case that shows us that a mother's love can be blinded by very human motives, for example, the desire to be rewarded, for prestige, and for status. The mother in our text and her two sons were very much concerned with the question of what discipleship was going to get them. Was it worthwhile to follow Christ? In other words, what was in it for them?

And this involved something else, for where compensation and reward are concerned the business of jealousy most certainly comes into play. Am I getting the "short end of the stick"? What kind of price do I set on my services?

The two brothers and their mother were firmly convinced that at the very least they deserved ranking posts in Jesus' kingdom, positions of prominence at the Master's left and his right.

And when the other disciples saw how ambitious these two brothers were, jealousy took hold of them. I can well imagine that they recalled their old question about which one of them was the greater (Matt. 18:1). Indeed, the desire for rank always unleashes the ugly forces of jealousy.

This passage shows us just how human even those who were closest to Jesus could be. They knew each other quite well—one might even say painfully well. Professional Christians are no exception; I mean those who stand in their pulpits and preach about love and unselfishness. Indeed, they are the most glaring examples of how jealousy and the craving for prestige can creep into and subvert human hearts. Who of them, many a preacher must wonder, draws the largest congregations to hear his sermons? Is it I? Or is it Pastor X? Or is it Pastor Y? Or is it Pastor Z? If it is the other fellow, then I have to struggle with all kinds of jealousy. I ask if perhaps my competitor does not attract more listeners than I do because of his demagogic, popular preaching style, whereas I am too intellectual and offer much more spiritual meat to my listeners. Perhaps I am really the more successful. And if that be the case, I tend to become very cocky.

One way or the other, am I filled with the dedication of a physician of souls that have been bought at a great price? Or am I concerned only with using my mind and rhetorical skills to move people and to make money out of what was achieved by the cross and humility? Everyone looks for a chance to denigrate another, to show up the bad side of his character. And what a joy it is to discover a rival's clay feet and to see him fall on his face! Whole columns and pages of our newspapers and magazines—particularly the sensational rags—draw their appeal from these instincts. These background motives are especially titillating when what Jesus suffered and died for is used as a springboard for our vanity, as, for example, when his disciples ask what they will get out of following him.

At the very outset we can see the contrast between the upward striving of the two brothers and the downward reaching of the Lord's love. One immediately suspects that the mother of these two disciples had boasted about her sons and advanced their cause before and that now she is again doing something foolish. Certainly Jesus, who knew men's hearts, knew that she was up to something foolish. And yet Jesus did not rebuke her impudence as so much foolish chatter.

How it must annoy God when his ears are assailed by such nonsense. I think, for example, of the prayers of the goalies of the two opposing teams at a soccer match, or of two nations at war with each other who try to win the Almighty over to their side. Or take, for example, the conflicting prayers offered in the course of electoral contests. I think of a certain political race in our German "Bible belt." When word got around that one side had organized a prayer fellowship in order to elect its candidate the other party organized a similar group. Thus, two political groups were aligned against each other in prayer. Jesus not only listens to such nonsense he even encourages it. Even though—humanly speaking—it is simpler to say "Shut up!" the Lord just says: "You do not realize what you are asking. You neither see what your prayer requires nor the consequences of what you desire. You actually do not know what it is for which you are asking." Later on, as he hangs upon the cross, he will say of his executioners, "They do not know what they are doing."

Without a doubt Jesus does not mean this as if to say: "It were better if you had never said this." Nor does he mean: "Your unawareness of what you are saying makes you an incompetent." No! When Jesus says "You do not know what you are doing," he is speaking to his executioners the forgiveness of his father. In our story Jesus uses this piece of maternal ambition, so thoughtlessly spoken, helpfully and pastorally to penetrate to the roots of these vanities on the soil on which they flourish and lovingly to uncover

them and to lead this mother and her sons to a "godly grief"
(2 Cor. 7:10). He does it because such a request as the one made
by Mrs. Zebedee is one which must be dealt with with all cards laid
face up on the table. I find it very comforting that with this Lord
we do not need to make our hearts a "den of thieves" but that we
can dare to tell God everything. And when sin creeps into our
prayers, when our prayers are filled with egoism and vanity, our
prayers are not negated because the forgiving love of our Father—
who at times is serious and who at times must be convulsed with
laughter—sees to it that even our foolishness does not separate us
from him. And it is precisely in the act of praying that our nonsense
comes to light. God does not expect us to pray the kind of prayers
that are filled with the wisdom of the ages and are carefully for-
mulated, polished, and edited for publication in our prayer books.
Our prayer is not purified and cleansed by omitting and suppress-
ing this or that. In the eyes of Jesus the roots of prayer that reach
into the aberrational are laid bare and dried up. I can almost imagine that old Mrs. Zebedee had no sooner spoken her request than
she bit her tongue. In that moment when we have spoken our
prayer in the presence of God and in the name of Jesus, we have
to revise and modify our prayer. If a prayer is genuinely sincere,
we must walk away from it differently than when we entered it—
indeed, perhaps than when we just fell into it.

How else can we risk asking God for anything?

Do we know what it is we are asking of God when we pray? Every
request we make of God is qualified to the extent that it must be
interpreted by the situation out of which we pray. Perhaps we are
in the situation of someone who is critically ill and we ask for healing
because we think recovery is good for us. But God knows (although
we do not) that we really need the illness. We could cite numerous
other instances from real life.

But no matter! We should talk with God comfortably, as dear
children speak with a loving father. For that reason we may pray
even about things that make us ashamed. We could not do that if
we had to weigh every word. Then we would have only the righteousness of the law. Humanly speaking, to do such a thing would
be to cultivate the old wisdom and to admit what is contrary to God
by the back door. In the process that begins with our petition and

ends with God's granting or denial of it, we will—as in our story—
undergo a kind of purification of our petitions and come to know
our hearts as they really are.

We see how this happens from the conversation between Jesus
and his two ambitious disciples. When Jesus tells them that achiev-
ing the high post they seek is no simple matter, that it involves
bitter cups of woe, they reply rather outspokenly: "We know that."
They are almost as flippant as Peter, who attributed to himself what
was necessary. Then Jesus leads them to a purification of their
wishes, of what they envisage as their goal as well as of their methods
to achieve that goal. We see that on a number of levels. Jesus does
not deny that they are ready and able to bear these hardships.

But what does that mean? If they at least know that hardship is
involved? How is it going to overtake him? Why must he suffer?

They do not know. Obviously they are thinking about the kind
of suffering that one must pay for with successes, as did the Mac-
cabees (2 Macc. 7:37) when they accepted their sufferings. They
suffered in order to accomplish something. They expected to be
compensated appropriately.

Obviously there are many kinds of sacrifice. Some sacrifice is a
means to an end, for example, to achieve some prominence in
heaven. That was the concern of Mrs. Zebedee and her sons. There
is also the suffering of Jesus, which is a sacrifice for others. His
entire life is nothing but pure service and sacrifice for others. He
intercedes for fallen man with his whole being, as Julius Schniewind
once put it. He offers his life as a ransom to secure a new freedom
for his brother—man.

Are these two brothers prepared to drink of the cup? Are they
willing to participate in the Lord's sufferings? Or will they turn
back when they find that a cup of endless failure is involved, a cup
that does not speculate in compensation and expectations?

From that there proceeds a second level of maturity: that he who
trusts in Jesus' Father alone in suffering and sacrifice ceases to
count the cost. Such a one lives from trust, and that is the absolute
opposite of counting. He leaves the whole matter of elevation in
God's hands.

That is what Jesus means when he says to the two brothers that
such things will be determined by his Father (Matt. 20:23). In this

sense the word "sacrifice" means—contrary to the idea of a means to an end, which is how those disciple-brothers thought—to leave such matters in God's hands to do with as he sees fit and proper. Reinhold Schneider quotes Johannes Tauler (1300–1361): "What does God want to accomplish through human suffering? That a man submit to the divine will" (cf. Ecclus. 2:1–11).

Finally, there is a third stage of maturity. Jesus gives these brothers to understand that they are harboring very earthly, very worldly desires and want to rule and belong to an elite group "up there." That is not meant in a derogatory way, as if there were no upper or lower distinctions in this life. Among Jesus' followers, however, it is a matter of other laws and structures. He who invests his life here must show very clearly by his conduct that we experience a new sense to our life—the sense of serving love and consequently of being there for others. Only in this way can one pray with Jesus (Matt. 11:25): "I thank thee, Father, Lord of heaven and earth, that thou hast hidden these things from the wise and understanding and revealed them to babes." Only he who no longer wants to be wisest and most prudent or most powerful, but who, with all the intellectual gifts he may possess regards himself as someone who has nothing to offer, who can only say "Lord, you are everything," only such a one can be the most lowly and serving; only such a one can go to Golgotha as a disciple.

Whoever follows the crucified Lord in the sacrifice of his life will probably have to lose his life, be held in contempt, be treated as an outsider in this life; and yet in all of this such a person will be certain of another kind of elevation than these brothers ever imagined. Such a one will trust that Jesus says to him as he assured the thief on the cross: "Today you shall be with me in Paradise."

Where is Paradise? Is it at Christ's left hand or at his right? What does it matter if the two brothers run the course of discipleship? Now everything depends on the promise of Jesus: "Today you will be with me in Paradise." "With me," and that in itself is paradise.

CHAPTER 18

Prayer—The Way
to Peace

In that day you will ask nothing of me. Truly, truly, I say
to you, if you ask anything of the Father he will give it to
you in my name. Hitherto you have asked nothing in my
name; ask, and you will receive, that your joy may be full.
. . . The hour is coming, indeed it has come, when you
will be scattered, every man to his home, and will leave
me alone; yet I am not alone, for the Father is with me.
I have said this to you, that in me you may have peace.
In the world you have tribulation; but be of good cheer,
I have overcome the world.

John 16:23–24, 32–33

There is more praying in this world than we think—and not only
among Christians but among atheists and agnostics as well. But our
text is not concerned with that. Our text is concerned with how we
pray.

We know from experience how to pray. All too often we just
chatter nonsense when we pray and say nothing: we babble the
kind of prayers that barely reach the ceiling much less the throne
of God! And how grateful we are when we really pray! How that
brightens the day and stays with us.

The word "Jesus" tells us how to pray. Real prayer has to do
with the "Name" Jesus. What does that mean? That name occurs
twice here: at the entrance of our prayer, so to speak, and again
at its exit or conclusion, where we wait to see what God will do with
what is in our heart. For one thing, the name "Jesus" means that
I come before God as one who prays in the name of Jesus, that is,

I am empowered by him to pray and to call upon God. What God grants us as the fulfillment of our petition he does in the name of Jesus, that is, for Jesus' sake.

I am afraid that that sort of thing could sound too much like an incantation, something in which we somehow find the secret of life.

To do this it is perhaps best to make clear what is not meant to pray in the name of Jesus. Let me give two extreme examples. In one of our old German hymn books was a chorale which went:

> Give rain, O Lord, and sunshine too
> To hoary aged, and callow youth;
> And whatever others else may crave
> Then let them ask of thee themselves.

This reminds me of another prayer that people used to pray when they were in dread of lightning, thunder, and even hail:

> O Blessed Saint Florian,
> Spare our homes from fire and flame
> Let others' homes catch fire instead.

In both cases the prayers are egoistic and provincial. In both cases the blessings of sunshine and protection which are implored are restricted to the little area of one's own most immediate vicinity. Such a prayer was intended for Bavarians, not for Hamburg, or Bremer. Least of all could such a prayer be meant for the tortured souls of Northern Ireland, the dissidents of the Soviet Union, or the refugees of Vietnam. We cannot pray in the Name of Jesus if we think only of ourselves and our own needs while we exclude all others from our prayer, those many others for whom Jesus also wants to be Savior.

One more example of how we can impede the name of Jesus. In Theodor Fontane's novel, *Count Petoefy*, the count speaks of the great anxiety that he experienced as a child during a storm blowing from the northwest. Every year such a seasonal storm would tear up trees and houses and overflow dams so that they could not hold back the onrushing floods. Of this childhood experience the count reports: "Yes, then we would pray, but we didn't know what we were saying because we were not thinking about God and faith. We were thinking only about our own need and danger and our soul was concerned with nothing but our anxiety and listening to the storm."

The count also reports that he was under the dreadful power of that against which he prayed. Our praying became a kind of conversation with ourselves about the things of which we are afraid. The anxiety we have in the world did not reach the one who has overcome the world. Rather, our prayer was spoken by one who was gripped by anxiety. The anxiety sucked the prayer into a strudel, as it were. Even Peter was filled with anxiety by the waves in which he was sinking so that he was no longer calling upon the Lord who is Master of all elements (Matt. 14:30). Even he had not stepped upon the waves in "the name of Jesus."

The objects of our prayer often can crowd out the very one to whom we want to pray. In the air-raid shelters during the war we were so horrified and filled with terror by the explosion of bombs and later by the sight of burning buildings that almost our every compulsion to pray was choked within us.

In what circumstances do we find the disciples depicted in our text? They are headed for a scattering, an hour when the Lord will leave them alone and cut off all connection with them; where, for that reason, anxiety and depression will overtake them. By what means could they withstand this force; what guidance to prayer could be recommended?

First let me say in the negative that it strikes me as quite characteristic that Jesus does not come to them with a demand: he makes a little exercise of concentration (in modern speech we would call it autogenic training) by means of which to flee from fixation with what threatens and to contemporize the presence of the Lord. Here it is necessary to hear what Jesus says of himself: I am not alone; even if you forsake me.

If we concentrate our thoughts on the Lord, then his relationship to us is very real to us. We know that he is in solidarity with us, that he has become our brother and that he shares our joy, our sorrow, our human fate. We are reminded of Melanchthon's phrase that expresses this bond with Christ in this way: "To recognize Christ is to recognize his good deeds upon us." We know who Christ is only when we understand him as "Christ for us." By itself this statement can make us overlook something quite decisive, indeed, it can even blind us to the fact that Christ achieves this brotherly relationship to us only because he has a unique relationship to his Father. If we do not consider this his inmost secret there is no use to chatter and pratter about solidarity and the brotherhood of man. Then that would all be nothing but what we experience in the case of a tragic hero in a play, someone whom we can identify, a hero who vicariously represents our human destiny. Jesus' entire life is grounded in his Father. "I came from the Father and have come into the world; again, I am leaving the world and going to the Father" (John 16:28); "yet I am not alone" even if you forsake me, "for the Father is with me" (John 16:32). In an even stronger quotation we can hear the Johannine Christ say: "I and the Father are one" (John 10:30). That is why there is peace in him; that is why his solidarity with us has redeeming power with us. When we find him, and pray in his name, we participate in this union with the Father. As long as we are with Jesus nothing can stand between us and God: we can really talk with him as children talk to a loving Father. Then there is peace.

To pray in the name of Jesus, then, means to call upon that which Jesus is for us: he has opened for us the access to God because he is one with the Father and turns himself to us with his whole being. The veil of the temple is torn. We have access to the Holiest of Holies. We are no longer closed out.

For the disciples who heard that, all of this is just so much futuristic whistling. The immediacy of this access is not opened to them. It is still a time of indirect communication hidden in parable and symbolism (Matt. 16:25). Only for a matter of moments is the veil torn away; only for a moment does the Lord appear in the glory toward which he is going. Yet, before all is made known, before Jesus' mission comes to an end, there has to be a leave-taking, a farewell. Jesus is giving some of his farewell discourse here. First Jesus must keep his promise that he will send the Comforter, the Paraclete, so that through him, he can be present with us in an entirely new way.

So, then, prayer in the name of Jesus means that, in the midst of all anxiety and abandonment, all confusion and loneliness, we hold onto him who stands at our side; one who is with the Father and who makes us certain that we are loved precisely there where gentle ones of this world are placed and where he dwells who rules all things and has power over every fate. "Will God not give us all things with him" (Rom. 8:32)?

So it cannot be otherwise than that he will be the "master of our joy," as Johann Franck called him. To me he is like a lighted window that shines in the night and promises security after all my aimless wandering through the dark valleys and bleak and barren mountain crags of this life!

> Give way vile spirits of gloom
> The master of my joy,
> Jesus the Lord is here!
> What joy is their's
> Who love God!